PRACTICAL

CHRISTIANITY

Old Testament Principles
——— *for* ———
Our New Life in Christ

From the Bible-Teaching Ministry of

Charles R. Swindoll

INSIGHT FOR LIVING

Insight for Living's Bible teacher, Chuck Swindoll, has devoted his life to the clear, practical application of God's Word and His grace. A pastor at heart, Chuck has served as senior pastor to congregations in Texas, Massachusetts, and California. He currently leads Stonebriar Community Church in Frisco, Texas, but Chuck's listening audience extends far beyond a local church body. As a leading program in Christian broadcasting, *Insight for Living* airs in major Christian radio markets, through more than 2,100 outlets worldwide, in 16 languages, and to a growing webcast audience. Chuck's extensive writing ministry has also served the body of Christ worldwide, and his leadership as president and now chancellor of Dallas Theological Seminary has helped prepare and equip a new generation for ministry. Chuck and Cynthia, his partner in life and ministry, have four children and ten grandchildren.

Based on the original outlines, charts, and transcripts of Charles R. Swindoll's sermons, these messages were originally presented in the Sunday evening worship services as practical Old Testament applications of the messages presented on Sunday mornings from the book of James. The original series included all the messages in the James series along with the practical Old Testament applications.

Editor in Chief:	**Editor:**
Cynthia Swindoll	Amy LaFuria
Study Guide Writer:	**Rights and Permissions:**
Mark Tobey	The Meredith Agency
Senior Editor and Assistant Writer:	**Text Designer:**
Wendy Peterson	Gary Lett
Editor and Assistant Writer:	**Typesetter:**
Marla DeShong	Bob Haskins

In 2001 the Old Testament messages were separated from the James series, and some additional sermons were added to form the current series titled *Practical Christianity: Old Testament Principles for Our New Life in Christ*. The study guide text was primarily taken from the *James* study guide coauthored in 1991 by Lee Hough, a graduate of The University of Texas at Arlington and Dallas Theological Seminary. In 2001 these chapters were revised by the Pastoral Ministries Department of Insight for Living.

Unless otherwise identified, all Scripture references are from the New American Standard Bible, © The Lockman Foundation 1960, 1962, 1963, 1968, 1971, 1972, 1973, 1975, 1977, 1995. Used by permission. Scripture taken from the Holy Bible, New International Version, Copyright © 1973, 1978, 1984 International Bible Society, used by permission of Zondervan Bible Publishers [NIV].

Portions of chapter 2 were adapted from the message "Growing through Loss, Job 1–2," chapter 4 of the study guide *Growing Pains*, coauthored by Lee Hough in 1991 and revised by Wendy Peterson and Jason Shephard. (Fullerton, Calif.: Insight for Living, 1999.)

Portions of chapter 9 were adapted from the message "Discovering the Missing Jewel of Worship, Isaiah 6:1–8," chapter 4 in the study guide *Making New Discoveries*, coauthored by Gary Matlack. (Fullerton, Calif.: Insight for Living, 1995.)

An effort has been made to locate sources and obtain permission where necessary for the quotations used in this book. In the event of any unintentional omission, a modification will gladly be incorporated in future printings.

ISBN 1-57972-375-6
Cover design: Alex Pasieka
Cover image: © Dan Lim/Masterfile
Printed in the United States of America

CONTENTS

INTRODUCTION

O ne tiny, three-letter word in the English Bible packs a powerful punch. The word is *all*. Because the languages of the Bible tend to be more precise than our English language, we know Scripture includes no throw-away words. The word *all* is no exception.

One of my favorite verses in the New Testament where this little dynamo appears is 2 Timothy 3:16:

> *All* Scripture is inspired by God and profitable for teaching, for reproof, for correction, for training in righteousness; so that the man of God may be adequate, equipped for every good work. (vv. 16–17, emphasis added)

There it is! Do you see the significance? *All* Scripture. *All* would include the Old Testament. Sadly, many believers today have a diminished appreciation for the practical value of the Hebrew Scriptures. They simply don't feel the Old Testament is relevant. To them, it seems out of touch with the issues of modern living.

Practical Christianity: Old Testament Principles for Our New life in Christ illustrates the power and relevance of the Old Testament for today's Christian. Using stories of real-life individuals from the Old Testament and how they faced life's daunting odds, I offer practical insights that will prove to be valuable to your walk with Christ.

Please join me on a journey to an ancient past not much different from our own. Hopefully, we will learn how to trust God and follow Christ by studying the struggles and triumphs of people like us.

Charles R. Swindoll

Charles R. Swindoll

PUTTING TRUTH INTO ACTION

K nowledge apart from application falls short of God's desire for His children. He wants us to apply what we learn so that we will change and grow. This Bible study guide was prepared with these goals in mind. As you go through the following pages, we hope your desire to discover biblical truth will grow as your understanding of God's Word increases and that you will be encouraged to apply what you've learned.

To assist you in your study, we've included a section called **Living Insights** at the end of each lesson. These exercises will challenge you to study further and to think of specific ways to put your discoveries into action.

On occasion a lesson is followed by a **Digging Deeper** section, which gives you additional information and resources to probe further into issues raised in that lesson.

There are many ways to use this guide—in personal devotions, group studies, discussions with friends and family, and Sunday School classes. And, of course, it's an ideal study aid when you're listening to its corresponding *Insight for Living* radio series.

To benefit most from this Bible study guide, we encourage you to consider it a spiritual journal. That's why we've included space in the **Living Insights** for recording your thoughts and discoveries. We hope you'll return to those sections often for review and encouragement as you continue to grow in your walk with Christ.

Insight for Living

PRACTICAL
CHRISTIANITY

Old Testament Principles
—— *for* ——
Our New Life in Christ

GETTING STARTED

What images come to your mind when you think of the Old Testament? Ancient scrolls with frayed yellow edges? A dusty collection of tales about Creation, Adam and Eve, floods and murder, giants and shepherd kings? Or, do you think of a list of rules and regulations that are hard to understand and even harder to obey?

Many Christians turn to the New Testament stories of Jesus and the disciples for fresh encouragement and practical help for life's challenges. The Old Testament just seems too distant and too far removed to have any real impact on our complicated, busy lives.

But the Old Testament is a magnificent tapestry of God's redemptive plan being worked out in the lives of real people who faced life's inevitable trials, just as we do. Some failed in their faith. Others triumphed in their trust. Most fell somewhere in between. Each one, however, came in contact with a loving, righteous God who offered them mercy and grace in their time of need.

The following four principles provide you with a clear Bible study method that will help you dig deeply into the Old Testament Scriptures and mine valuable treasures of truth. We hope that as you follow these steps, your appetite for the Old Testament will grow and you will be filled with satisfaction as you draw closer to God.

Once you choose a passage to study, the first step is *observation*. Write down your observations using the five W's: Who, What, Where, When, and Why. Here are some helpful questions to get you started: What does this passage *say*? Who are the main characters? What are they doing or saying? Why? What is the subject of the passage? Where is the action occurring? What is the time frame? What are the surrounding circumstances? What is the context?

The second step is *interpretation*. Take your written observations and interpret them by asking yourself: What does this passage *mean*? Why are the characters speaking or acting this way? What do their motives seem to be? What is going on behind the scenes? How is God interacting with them? Are they obeying Him? Why or why not?

The third step is *correlation*, also referred to as *integration*. Once you have recorded your observations and interpreted them, ask yourself: What is the theme of this passage? Is there a "moral" to the story? How does this passage fit with earlier and later events?

What sense can I make of it? What happened and what was the outcome? How did the characters change as a result? Try to create a cohesive whole out of the dialogue and events that are taking place. You will probably still have some questions. That's okay! Write them down.

The fourth step is *application*. This step asks the following vital questions: What does it mean to *me*? What principles from this passage are still applicable today? How can I apply them to my life? The best way to answer these questions is to focus on three key issues: knowledge, attitudes, and behavior.

Knowledge. This step of application focuses on what we have learned from the passage. Ask yourself: What are the new perspectives that I have gained? What have I learned about God, people, Scripture, and so on? What implications do its principles have for my everyday life—church, work, play, finances, family, friendships, and priorities? What do I understand now about God and His plan that I didn't understand before?

Attitudes. This step takes application from our heads to our hearts! Ask yourself: How does having this knowledge change my heart? How does it affect my attitudes toward life? How should I feel now about Christ, myself, my family, my friends, my job, and the world? How are my commitments, opportunities, and responsibilities impacted by these truths? In what areas do I need to adjust my attitudes as a result of what I have discovered in this passage?

Behavior. This step takes application from our hearts to our hands. It asks the questions: How does this affect the way I will *live* from now on? What strategies can I implement to bring these concepts into my life in a meaningful way? How have I changed, and how can I demonstrate this to others through my words and actions?

Remember that the Christian life was never designed to be lived in isolation. We need each other to help keep our lives balanced and our faith on target. Seek out a trusted friend to help keep you accountable to the truths you've been learning. And remember, Scripture always demands a response. We don't just need information; we need transformation!

You will be amazed by how meaningful and fulfilling your Bible study will become once you begin to use this straightforward method. If you'd like to go deeper still, we have suggested some additional resources for you in the *Books for Probing Further* section at the end of this guide.

Have a wonderful journey!

Chapter 1

MARKS OF A PRACTICAL CHRISTIAN

Psalm 15

In his continuation of C. S. Lewis' book *The Screwtape Letters*, Walter Martin zeroed in on one of the Devil's favorite schemes: turning Christianity into *churchianity*. As the demon Uncle Screwtape writes to his demonic nephew Wormwood:

> In this marvelous imitation of the Enemy's [Christ's] church everything looks and sounds right and good, but the Enemy's Spirit [the Holy Spirit] is conspicuously absent. You must arrange to make him a devout Methodist or Anglican or Baptist or Presbyterian or what have you. But he must come to accept the church as a type of religious social club where people congregate to be helped and to help each other (a splendid half-truth), not to be redeemed and instructed by the Enemy. . . .
>
> . . . In a word, help him to become more religious, but for hell's sake and your own, not more Christian![1]

What's the difference between being religious and being Christian? How can we tell if we've veered into *churchianity*—and how

---

1. Walter Martin, *Screwtape Writes Again* (Santa Ana, Calif.: Vision House Publishers, 1975), pp. 37–39.

1

do we correct our course and get back to God? We can begin by asking ourselves some questions:

- Am I focusing more on my own righteousness than on God's grace?

- Has church attendance become more important than a daily relationship with God?

- Do my actions show that I'm rooted and growing in God's holy love, or am I merely paying lip service to the Gospel's values?

In one of his psalms, David added another question—yes, David from the Old Testament. Obviously, religiosity has been one of Satan's most successful ploys for a long time! Here is David's question, with the second line echoing the first:

> O Lord, who may abide in Your tent?
> Who may dwell on Your holy hill?[2] (Ps. 15:1)

The rest of David's psalm contains the insights God gave him, and when we apply them to our lives, they will transpose the dissonant strains of dull religiosity into the harmonious expressions of genuine Christianity.

Rescued from Darkness to Walk in Light

Some people think that all there is to the Christian life is trusting Christ as one's Savior. Once you believe in Him, your spot is reserved in heaven, and that's all that matters, right? Wrong. As both the Old and New Testaments show, God's salvation ushers people into a whole new way of life—God's design for life.

Let's gain a solid understanding of what happens the moment we acknowledge Jesus Christ as our Savior—and how that shapes the rest of our lives.

The Moment We Believe

The instant we place our faith in Christ, we are *in Christ* (see Rom. 8:1; 1 Cor. 1:30; 2 Cor. 5:17; Gal. 3:26). Not only do we

---

2. The Hebrew images of a "tent" and a "holy hill" are symbolic, not literal. Both idioms refer to the place of God's presence, of spiritual intimacy. In a poetic way, David was asking, "What kind of person can dwell in God's holy presence? Who can maintain intimate fellowship with the Lord?" In essence, he wondered what distinguished someone who has religion from someone who has a relationship with God (compare the imagery in Ps. 91:1).

have an eternal inheritance in heaven, but we are forgiven of all our sins, justified and accepted by God, regenerated, free from sin's tyranny and Satan's domain, adopted as the Lord's own children, reconciled and at peace with God, and forever secure in the salvation He has purchased for us with His Son's own life (see 1 Pet. 1:18–19; Jude 24–25).

Our salvation is permanent—it never changes—because God alone has established it (see Eph. 2:8). No amount of work on our part was required (see v. 9). We may not always feel like we're forgiven, justified, freed, at peace, and adopted, but God sees and knows what's invisible to us (see 2 Cor. 4:18; 5:7).

The Lord gives us all these benefits at the moment of belief, but this is only the beginning. Just as babies don't stay babies but grow to become mature adults, so we, after we're born again, need to grow up and mature in Christ.

The Rest of Our Lives

This process of growing up is called *sanctification* (see Rom. 6:19; 1 Thess. 5:23). While salvation *moves us into Christ*, sanctification happens because *Christ is in us* (see John 17:22–23; Rom. 8:10; Gal. 2:20). His Holy Spirit dwells in our hearts, helping us give Christ control over our lives so that we

- experience greater power in prayer.

- bear more of the Spirit's fruit.

- deepen our hunger for God's Word.

- give ourselves more fully in worship.

- more readily obey the Lord's will.

- witness to others with deeper compassion and understanding.

- increase in wisdom and insight.

Unlike our salvation, our sanctification can be impacted by our actions. When we cooperate with the Spirit's work in our lives, we will grow in the areas listed above. We'll have a deeper fellowship with the Lord and begin to look more like His Son. If we resist the Spirit, however, choosing our will over God's, our spiritual growth will be stunted. We'll hinder the process of maturity—and it will show.

Salvation is just the initial downbeat in the magnificent symphony Christ wants to compose with our lives. We are meant to be His *magnum opus* in progress. As Paul wrote to the Ephesians:

> For we are His workmanship, created in Christ Jesus
> for good works, which God prepared beforehand so
> that we would walk in them. (2:10)

The Lord's values and ethics are the same in the New Testament as they were in the Old. This is why we can learn about our walk with Christ from His servant David and gain some very practical insights into the good works God has prepared for His people.

Portrait of a Godly Life

In Psalm 15, David painted a detailed portrait of the person who loves the living Lord rather than a religion. Let's look at the particulars of such a person's character, speech, and actions.

Taking the Moral High Road

David wrote that someone who dwells in God's presence is:

> He who walks with integrity, and works righteousness,
> And speaks truth in his heart. (v. 2)

The Hebrew term translated *integrity* means "complete . . . full, whole, upright."[3] Those who want to live in the Lord's presence have no hidden sins kept under lock and key in some shadowy corner of their lives. Their walk, or way of life, harmonizes with God's standards. From a heart of love and reverence, they deeply desire to please God (see 2 Cor. 5:9; Eph. 5:10; Col. 1:10).[4] And they leave a lasting legacy of blessing behind them (see Prov. 20:7).

Overly-religious people, in contrast, usually try to be moral perfectionists. Their morality becomes their god, and love for the Lord and other people gets squeezed out by the pressure to perform. In a family setting, for example, a legalistic parent might inject discord into the home through criticism, mistrust, and anger. But a parent whose moral integrity is fueled by a love for God can live transparently before others, which will foster peaceful harmony in the home.

David next singled out the quality of righteousness (Ps. 15:2).

3. R. Laird Harris, Gleason L. Archer, Jr., and Bruce K. Waltke, eds., *Theological Wordbook of the Old Testament* (Chicago, Ill.: Moody Press, 1980), vol. 2, pp. 973–74.

4. Willem A. VanGemeren, "Psalms," in *The Expositor's Bible Commentary,* ed. Frank E. Gaebelein (Grand Rapids, Mich.: Zondervan Publishing House, 1991), vol. 5, p. 150.

People who actively "work righteousness" are "in a right relationship to God, [and do] what God would do," because their hearts are "turned towards God and not towards . . . self."[5] Because Christ secured our righteous standing with God (Rom. 3:21–26), we're now freed from sin and can draw clear boundaries between what's godly and what's not. As we grow in the Lord, He helps us become more ethical, honest, and straightforward in our daily conduct.

Those who "speak the truth in their hearts" are people whose inner lives match their outward lives. As David wrote in another psalm, "Behold, You desire truth in the innermost being" (51:6a). The stuff found deep within the human soul (the heart) determines true character, as Jesus taught:

> "For the mouth speaks out of that which fills the heart. The good man brings out of his good treasure what is good; and the evil man brings out of his evil treasure what is evil." (Matt. 12:34b–35)

If we wish to truly dwell in the Lord's presence, we can't get by on lip service. There must not be a credibility gap between our hearts and our tongues—what we say must reflect who we are.

Using Words to Help, Not Hurt

Next, David shifted his focus from the language of the heart to the way it is translated on the tongue of the person who abides with God.

> He does not slander with his tongue,
> Nor does evil to his neighbor,
> Nor takes up a reproach against his friend. (Ps. 15:3)

The word *slander* literally means "to go about on foot." The more conventional meaning is "to gossip." Picture a person who would "play the spy"—sneak into someone's home, gather information, then maliciously distort and gossip about it with others. If you've ever been lied about, you know the pain of having your reputation damaged by people who don't even care.

Godly people, however, do care about the truth, because God is the Lord of truth (Isa. 65:16). They work to build others up

---

5. George A. F. Knight, *Psalms*, The Daily Study Bible Series (Philadelphia, Pa.: Westminster Press, 1982), vol. 1, p. 71.

instead of tear them apart because this reflects God's love. As another psalmist, Ethan, wrote:

> Righteousness and justice are the foundation of
> Your throne;
> Lovingkindness and truth go before You. (Ps. 89:14)

Genuinely spiritual people recognize that slandering someone else is a deep, evil offense against God, and they refuse to do it. David uses the word *neighbor*, which actually means "friend, companion, fellow." In our relationships with others, we're directed to treat everyone with the same care we would give to our friends. And friends don't "take up a reproach," or cast slurs, on the character of someone they're close to (compare Lev. 19:16–18).

Celebrating the Lord Rather than Laughing at Sin

> In whose eyes a reprobate is despised,
> But who honors those who fear the Lord. (Ps. 15:4a)

What kind of person is a "reprobate"? Someone who rejects or despises[6] the Lord. A reprobate is also a "perpetual undertaker of evil"[7] because he or she pours contempt on God's values. According to David, the godly person despises the despiser of God.

Now, before we go too far with this idea, let's understand what David meant in this context. To despise doesn't mean we should hate nonbelievers, treat them with contempt, or attack them. Rather, we are wise to avoid "the company and influence of evil persons."[8] In contrast, godly people "honor those who fear the Lord"—they value the "companionship and positive influence"[9] of those who love and reverence God.

An obvious birthmark of real Christianity is showing genuine support, appreciation, and gratitude for others—especially those who exalt the Lord and walk according to His ways. As Paul wrote in his letter to the Romans, "Let love be without hypocrisy. Abhor what is evil [notice, it does not say "*who* is evil"]; cling to what is

---

6. See Harris, Archer, and Waltke, *Theological Wordbook of the Old Testament*, vol. 1, p. 488.

7. Peter C. Craigie, *Word Biblical Commentary: Psalms 1–50* (Waco, Tex.: Word Books, Publisher, 1983), vol. 19, p. 152.

8. Craigie, *Psalms 1–50*, p. 152.

9. Craigie, *Psalms 1–50*, p. 152.

good. Be devoted to one another in brotherly love; give preference to one another in honor" (12:9–10; see also 1 Pet. 1:22).

Keeping One's Word—No Matter What

> He swears to his own hurt and does not change.
> (Ps. 15:4b)

A godly person's promise is something people can count on. The genuine Christian "has a deep sense of integrity and must often make material sacrifices to be honest. His honor is more important than his wallet."[10] Some simple but easily overlooked ways of living the truth of this verse are keeping our word, showing up for appointments (on time), and following through with commitments. In the eyes of others, our credibility—and frankly, the credibility of the Gospel—depends on our ability to do what we say we will do.

Valuing People More Than Money

> He does not put out his money at interest,
> Nor does he take a bribe against the innocent.
> (v. 5a)

Those who love God don't put personal profit at the center of their lives. Remember what Jesus told us? "No one can serve two masters; for either he will hate the one and love the other, or he will be devoted to one and despise the other. You cannot serve God and wealth" (Matt. 6:24). If we devote ourselves to the getting and keeping of money, we'll put little stock in God's values. But if we're sold out to God, then we'll also invest in His people and their needs.

Commentator Allen Ross notes that David's first phrase is especially vivid in Hebrew: "he does not put the bite on them."[11] At one time or another, we've all smarted from the teeth marks left by those who have bitten down on us financially. So we should not unleash ravenous interest rates on loans to those in need, especially other Christians (see Lev. 25:35–38; Deut. 23:19–20). Someone whose heart beats in rhythm with God's is prompted to assist someone in need not by a desire to take advantage, but by a loving desire to help.

---

10. VanGemeren, "Psalms," pp. 14–15.

11. Allen P. Ross, "Psalms," in *The Bible Knowledge Commentary*, Old Testament edition, ed. John F. Walvoord and Roy B. Zuck (Colorado Springs, Colo.: Chariot Victor Publishing, 1985), p. 803.

Likewise, when a person is in need of justice, those who truly care about God's values set personal gain aside to make sure that the righteous cause of a person is upheld. In antiquity, a poor man was powerless to defend himself against wealthy businessmen who paid expensive bribes to twist the courts to rule in their favor. This mangled form of injustice was strictly prohibited by Jewish law and condemned vehemently by the prophets (see Exod. 23:6–8; Deut. 16:19–20; Isa. 1:23; 5:23; Amos 5:11–15). Authentic Christians devote themselves to justice, letting it "roll down like waters" (Amos 5:24).

Promise to the Godly

David closes with God's wonderful promise to the one whose walk with Him reflects these traits:

> He who does these things will never be shaken.
> (Ps. 15:5b)

Like a mighty oak standing undaunted by fierce winds, the believer who abides with the Lord cannot be uprooted. When we experience real intimacy with God, our roots grow deep into the soil of His presence, and we exchange our own frailties and weaknesses for His stability and strength.

So then, what kind of person can have the winds rage against their life and still keep their faith standing strong and true? Those who abide in God's presence—not the one who gets caught up in *churchianity*, but the one who dwells on the Lord's holy hill through living the very real, very practical life of faith described in Psalm 15.

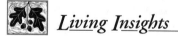 *Living Insights*

You've probably been applying this chapter to your life as you've studied it, so now sharpen your focus by putting your thoughts into words.

Are you living a life of genuine faith, or have you fallen into the comfortable trap of *churchianity*? What evidence do you see of one or the other? For example, do your actions and attitudes strike a sour note when measured by the score of God's Word?

_____

_____

_____

Of course, even in a genuine walk of faith, we're still human, and we still make mistakes. In which area or areas that David addressed do you need the Lord's transforming touch: Speaking the truth in your heart? Not tearing others down with your words? Allowing your life to be more influenced by those who respect God than those who don't? Keeping your word? Helping those in need without looking for what you can get out of it? Write down your thoughts as the Holy Spirit leads you.

_____

_____

_____

Take these areas to the Lord in prayer right now. Ask Him where you should start in retuning your heart to His Word. What can you do as a first step? For example, do you need to apologize to anyone? Do you need to come to terms with a tendency toward denial? What will your next step be?

_____

_____

_____

As you experience the Lord's presence in your life each day—not just on Sundays—your intimacy with Him will become more natural. And when He takes up His baton, you'll be ready for your cue in His symphony of life—to play in harmony with the Master!

 *Questions for Group Discussion*

1. Review Psalm 15 together. Take some time to discuss the psalm-ist's use of imagery. What are the most vivid images you see? How do they help you understand the meaning of the psalm?

2. How do the images *tent* and *holy hill* help you grasp the significance of the Lord's presence? What historical references may be in view? Now read the first few verses of Psalm 91. How are these two psalms similar? How are they different?

3. If Psalm 15 was, in fact, sung by ancient Jewish pilgrims on their way to worship in Jerusalem, what would have been the significance of this song? What sorts of things can believers do today to help prepare themselves to enter the Lord's presence? What role does music play in preparing people for worship?

4. What New Testament passages correlate with the principles for godliness described in Psalm 15? Try to summarize the message of Psalm 15 as it relates to your relationship with Jesus Christ.

Chapter 2

HOW TO TRUST WHEN YOU'RE TROUBLED

Job 1–2:10

How did you start *your* day today? With a leap and a bound, planting both feet firmly on the floor? Or did you roll over with a groan, cursing the banter of morning radio hosts bleating from your alarm, dreading the light of day?

If it was the latter, maybe you stayed up too late the night before—or maybe it's more serious than that. Maybe fear, grief, or depression is draining your motivation and robbing you of your joy. Perhaps your trust in God has started to cave in under the pressure of your struggle, reducing your once long and heartfelt prayers to terse, sentence entreaties of desperate hurt.

If this is you, you're probably weary of well-intentioned people tossing platitudes at you like so much loose change: "Well, I'm sure it'll all work out," or "Remember, God works all things together for good," or "You need to go on with your life." You smile graciously in response, but inside you feel their glib words offer nothing more than a mirage of hope. They only salt your thirst for genuine comfort, and your heart cries out, "Lord, how long will I have to live like this? Will I ever feel Your presence again? Am I really going to make it through this? Are You really there—really loving me?" The questions are unrelenting.

How do we trust God when a trial has swallowed us whole? What do we do when we're mired in muddling doubts? How do we hold onto hope when the winds of adversity blast against us?

There are no easy answers, not even in the Bible. There is no magic verse we can wave over our lives to make pain disappear. But in God's Word we're given His wisdom—mainstays of His truth that secure us to Him when the barometer of life drops to the bottom of the gauge.

Many consider Job to be *the* textbook on how to handle suffering.

This chapter has been adapted from "Growing through Loss," from the Bible study guide *Growing Pains*, rev. ed., from the Bible-teaching ministry of Charles R. Swindoll (Anaheim, Calif.: Insight for Living, 1999).

But as Philip Yancey suggests, the point of Job "is not suffering . . . The point is faith: Where is Job when it hurts? How is he responding?"[1] In the first two chapters of the book of Job, Job makes an astonishing response to the avalanche of disasters that tore his life apart. Let's walk beside him and explore five extraordinary scenes from his life.

Five Scenes That Resulted in Calamity

The opening scene on earth provides a description of Job's walk with God, his wealth, and his warm family life (Job 1:1–5). God calls Job "blameless" and "upright," and Job is pictured praying and interceding for his ten children:

> There was a man in the land of Uz, whose name was Job; and that man was blameless, upright, fearing God and turning away from evil. Seven sons and three daughters were born to him. His possessions also were 7,000 sheep, 3,000 camels, 500 yoke of oxen, 500 female donkeys, and very many servants; and that man was the greatest of all the men of the east. His sons used to go and hold a feast in the house of each one on his day, and they would send and invite their three sisters to eat and drink with them. When the days of feasting had completed their cycle, Job would send and consecrate them, rising up early in the morning and offering burnt offerings according to the number of them all; for Job said, "Perhaps my sons have sinned and cursed God in their hearts." Thus Job did continually. (Job 1:1–5)

In scene two, the spotlight shifts from earth to heaven, and we're given a behind-the-scenes glimpse of the circumstances responsible for Job's suffering.

A Troubler in Heaven

> Now there was a day when the sons of God came to present themselves before the Lord, and Satan also came among them. The Lord said to Satan,

1. Philip Yancey, *Disappointment with God* (Grand Rapids, Mich.: Zondervan Publishing House, 1988), p. 165.

"From where do you come?" Then Satan answered the Lord and said, "From roaming about on the earth and walking around on it." The Lord said to Satan, "Have you considered My servant Job? For there is no one like him on the earth, a blameless and upright man, fearing God and turning away from evil." Then Satan answered the Lord, "Does Job fear God for nothing? Have You not made a hedge about him and his house and all that he has, on every side? You have blessed the work of his hands, and his possessions have increased in the land. But put forth Your hand now and touch all that he has; he will surely curse You to Your face." Then the Lord said to Satan, "Behold, all that he has is in your power, only do not put forth your hand on him." So Satan departed from the presence of the Lord. (vv. 6–12)

Job's in the dark—unaware Satan has wagered that, if pushed hard enough, this choice servant would actually curse God. Philip Yancey provides another helpful insight:

Yes, there was an arm wrestling match, but not between Job and God. Rather, *Satan* and God were the chief combatants, although—most significantly—God had designated the man Job as his stand-in. The first and last chapters make clear that Job was unknowingly performing in a cosmic showdown before spectators in the unseen world.[2]

With the backdrop for Job's fiery trial rolled into place, let's look at the third scene—Satan's all-out assault.

Catastrophe on Earth

Now on the day when his sons and daughters were eating and drinking wine in their oldest brother's house, a messenger came to Job and said, "The oxen were plowing and the donkeys feeding beside them, and the Sabeans attacked and took them. They also slew the servants with the edge of the sword, and I alone have escaped to tell you."

2. Yancey, *Disappointment with God*, p. 168.

While he was still speaking, another also came and said, "The fire of God fell from heaven and burned up the sheep and the servants and consumed them, and I alone have escaped to tell you." *While he was still speaking*, another came and said, "The Chaldeans formed three bands and made a raid on the camels and took them and slew the servants with the edge of the sword, and I alone have escaped to tell you." *While he was still speaking*, another also came and said, "Your sons and your daughters were eating and drinking wine in their oldest brother's house, and behold, a great wind came from across the wilderness and struck the four corners of the house, and it fell on the young people and they died, and I alone have escaped to tell you." (vv. 13–19, emphasis added)

Without warning, a tidal wave of Satan's fury crashed onto the placid shores of Job's life, sweeping everything he had out to sea. And the storm wasn't over yet. Let's see what happens in scene four from the life of Job.

Satan Not Satisfied

Again there was a day when the sons of God came to present themselves before the Lord, and Satan also came among them to present himself before the Lord. The Lord said to Satan, "Where have you come from?" Then Satan answered the Lord and said, "From roaming about on the earth and walking about on it." The Lord said to Satan, "Have you considered My servant Job? For there is no one like him on the earth, a blameless and upright man fearing God and turning away from evil. And he still holds fast his integrity, although you incited Me against him to ruin him without cause." Satan answered the Lord and said, "Skin for skin! Yes, all that a man has he will give for his life. However, put forth Your hand now, and touch his bone and his flesh; he will curse You to Your face." So the Lord said to Satan, "Behold, he is in your power, only spare his life." (2:1–6)

Not satisfied with wiping out Job's life's work and bereaving

14

him of his children, Satan hissed out his new scheme: "Skin for skin!" In the fifth scene, Satan would destroy Job's body to get at his soul.

Job's Agony Intensified

> Then Satan went out from the presence of the Lord and smote Job with sore boils from the sole of his foot to the crown of his head. And he took a potsherd to scrape himself while he was sitting among the ashes. (vv. 7–8)

As Job tried to stumble back to his feet, another wave of disaster knocked him back to the dust. Satan felt certain that the misery brought on by a debilitating disease would cripple even this most stalwart of souls. Still, Job's trust in God did not waver, much to Satan's chagrin.

Four Responses That Revealed Integrity

Job, now alone in his misery, embodied despair as he sat scratching the open sores oozing from his skin. However, his deep resolve to trust God was evident in his responses to this devastating calamity.

Worship

When Satan retreated to see what his victim would do after the first round of calamities—hopefully, curse God—he was startled to witness Job holding fast to his adoration of the Lord:

> Then Job arose and tore his robe and shaved his head, and he fell to the ground and worshiped. (1:20)

Battered and worn by Satan's gratuitous assault, Job bowed in worship. Not only his body, but also his will, lay prostrate before the Lord. His head was shaved as bare as his life, and his clothes were as tattered as his heart. One Bible scholar observes, "Behold, the wise man! Not wise because he comprehended the mystery of his sufferings, but because, not comprehending, he feared God still."[3]

---

3. Charles F. Pfeiffer and Everett F. Harrison, eds., *The Wycliffe Bible Commentary*, (Chicago, Ill.: Moody Press, 1962), p. 462.

Humility

Satan waited for Job to speak, thinking his words would undoubtedly betray a festering bitterness toward God. However, Satan underestimated the strength of Job's faith. What came from Job's trembling lips was not cursing, but blessing:[4]

> "Naked I came from my mother's womb,
> And naked I shall return there.
> The Lord gave and the Lord has taken away.
> Blessed be the name of the Lord." (v. 21)

Job's hands did not need to be full before he could worship God. He settled that issue long before the tide began rising against him. Though faintly sung, Job's simple canticle revealed a humble surrender to God's sovereign but mysterious plan.

Silence

Another of Job's astonishing responses came just after Satan had afflicted him with boils. It is evident in what he chose not to do:

> And he took a potsherd to scrape himself while he
> was sitting among the ashes. (2:8)

He didn't say anything! Job's misery drove him to silence and the town's ash heap—"a collection of the ashes from the city's ovens, broken pots, and other refuse; it was the abode of outcasts."[5] His silent, humble grieving is remarkable when we consider the brutality of his illness:

> From Job's speeches some of the symptoms that he
> suffered included painful pruritus [severe itching]
> (2:8), disfiguration (2:12), purulent [pus-filled] sores
> that scab over, crack, and ooze (7:5), sores infected
> with worms (7:5), fever with chills (21:6; 30:30),
> darkening and shriveling of the skin (30:30), eyes

---

4. In the Hebrew there is an ironic play on the words *curse* (v. 11) and *bless* (v. 21). Both words come from the same root word, *barak*, but they have very different meanings. Satan crowed in verse 11, "He will surely curse You to Your face." And in verse 21 Job said, "Blessed be the name of the Lord." Satan used the word to promise blasphemy, but Job used it to deliver praise instead.

5. John E. Hartley, "The Book of Job," *The New International Commentary on the Old Testament*, ed. R. K. Harrison (Grand Rapids, Mich.: William B. Eerdmans Publishing Co., 1988), p. 83.

red and swollen from weeping (16:16), diarrhea (30:27), sleeplessness and delirium (7:4, 13–14), choking (7:15), bad breath (19:17), emaciation (19:20), and excruciating pain throughout his body (30:17).[6]

This was as violent and horrible an illness as anyone could imagine. But instead of shaking his fists at God, Job wrapped his pain in the gauze of silence. His wife was also struggling in her pain. Remember, she'd lost her children too. She, too, was impoverished, and now she had to watch helplessly as her husband suffered in physical agony. Her words, unfortunately, offered no comfort to Job:

> Then his wife said to him, "Do you still hold fast your integrity? Curse God and die!" (2:9)

Did she blame Job for the troubles that had befallen them? Had she lost her faith in God? Or was she seeking a mercifully quick end for her husband's pain? No one knows. Commentator John Hartley observes, "According to her view, to compromise one's faith in God in order to ease an intolerable burden is the wisest course to follow."[7] Her words only heaped more hurt on Job, alienating them from each other at a time when they most needed comfort and support.

Acceptance

How did Job answer his wife? Amazingly, he held fast to his faith, corrected her misguided counsel, and willingly accepted his miserable plight:

> But he said to her, "You speak as one of the foolish women speaks. Shall we indeed accept good from God and not accept adversity?" In all this Job did not sin with his lips. (2:10)

With this humble response, Job choked all remaining life from Satan's diabolic scheme. He simply would not be dissuaded from trusting God, regardless of how bleak life had become.

---

6. John E. Hartley, "The Book of Job," as quoted in the Bible study guide *Growing Pains*, rev. ed., written by Lee Hough, from the Bible-teaching ministry of Charles R. Swindoll (Anaheim, Calif.: Insight for Living, 1999), p. 33.

7. John E. Hartley, "The Book of Job," p. 84.

Three Reasons for Reinforced Stability

Before we end our journey with Job, let's consider how his faith withstood such intense testing.

From the passages we've studied, we see that *Job looked up and was comforted by God's sovereignty* (see Job 1:21; 2:10). Job could have easily concluded from his circumstances that God was capricious and cruel. Instead, he clung tenaciously to the comforting truth that God was in control of everything in his life. Though he did not understand *why* things were unfolding as they were, he found strength in believing that God knew best.

Job looked ahead and was reminded of God's presence (see Job 19:25–27). By faith, Job looked ahead with the assurance that one day he would rest safely in the presence of the Lord, at last free from every evil scheme of Satan.

At the end of his odyssey of pain, *Job looked around and was shaped by God's instruction* (see Job 42:1–6). We've only seen the beginning of Job's journey in this chapter, but under the excruciating pressure of his trials, Job's resolve eventually weakened. In the beginning, he sought God for an answer to the enigma of his circumstances. But soon this seeking changed to a demand for an explanation. Remarkably, God never really answered Job's questions but instead revealed His omnipotent control over all creation. In light of it all, Job said, "I repent in dust and ashes" (v. 6) and humbly submitted as clay to be molded by the Potter without reservation.

A Final Thought

Someone once said, "We are all faced with a series of great opportunities, brilliantly disguised as unsolvable problems." According to Yancey:

> For Job, the battleground of faith involved lost possessions, lost family members, lost health. We may face a different struggle: a career failure, a floundering marriage, sexual orientation, a body shape that turns people off, not on. At such times the outer circumstances—the illness, the bank account, the run of bad luck—will seem the real struggle. We may beg God to change those circumstances. *If only I were beautiful or handsome, then everything would work out. If only I had more money—or at least a job—then*

I could easily believe God.

But the more important battle, as shown in Job, takes place inside us. Will we trust God? Job teaches that at the moment when faith is hardest and *least* likely, then faith is most needed. . . .

. . . Every act of faith by every one of the people of God is like the tolling of a bell, and a faith like Job's reverberates throughout the universe.

Worship, humility, silence, and acceptance are the responses of faith Job used to help rise above the storm. Let your trust in God reverberate with the same responses today—no matter your circumstances. When you do, you'll see how they will strengthen your endurance and deepen your relationship with the Lord.

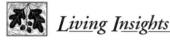 *Living Insights*

"I cry out to You for help, but You do not answer me;
I stand up, and you turn Your attention against
    me. . . .
You lift me up to the wind and cause me to ride;
And You dissolve me in a storm." (Job 30:20, 22)

Have you ever felt like Job—dissolved in the lashing rains of a storm? It may have seemed like God turned His back on you, but He doesn't do that to us—and He didn't do that to Job. As God showed through His Son, Jesus Christ, He stays close by when storms test our faith:

Now on one of those days Jesus and His disciples got into the boat, and He said to them, "Let us go over to the other side of the lake." So they launched out. But as they were sailing along He fell asleep; and a fierce gale of wind descended on the lake, and they began to be swamped and to be in danger. They came to Jesus and woke Him up, saying, "Master, Master, we are perishing!" And He got up and rebuked the wind and the surging waves, and they stopped, and it became calm. And He said to them,

8. Yancey, *Disappointment with God*, pp. 172–74.

"Where is your faith?" They were fearful and amazed, saying to one another, "Who then is this, that He commands even the winds and the water, and they obey Him?" (Luke 8:22–25)

This great story has striking parallels to Job's ordeal. What are some that you notice? For example, what circumstances of the disciples' test of faith remind you of Job's?

_____

_____

_____

_____

_____

_____

_____

Describe how you think the disciples may have felt as they realized their boat was about to sink. Have you ever felt that way in the middle of a trial? Are you feeling that way now? Why?

_____

_____

_____

_____

_____

_____

What role did fear play in the disciples' response to the storm? Was their fear warranted, or could it have been exaggerated? How does fear keep you from trusting the Lord's promises?

_____

_____

_____

_____

_____

_____

_____

Jesus first met the disciples' perceived need, which was relief from the threatening storm. He then turned their attention to a deeper need—their lack of faith. Though thoroughly enjoying the benefits of His acquaintance, they were not prepared to trust Christ when life got a little dicey.

How about you? To what degree do you believe Jesus will see you through your difficult times? What truths from our study of Job could help stretch your threshold of faith?

_____

_____

_____

_____

_____

_____

Carve out some time to spend in prayer with the Savior. Since He already knows every detail about the trial staring you down, ask Him for wisdom to help keep your faith from flinching. Then, thank Him for the grace and strength He freely gives . . . especially when you've got nothin' but trouble.

 *Questions for Group Discussion*

1. Discuss some of the trials you and members of your group face today. How are they similar to Job's? How do they differ? Are there Job-like responses missing from the mix?

2. What lessons about God have you gleaned from Job's story? What did you learn about Satan? Do you feel Satan still acts in sinister ways, tempting believers to doubt their faith? Explain.

3. A major theme in Job is suffering. Discuss your understanding of the role suffering plays in the life of the Christian. Is suffering always part of God's plan for spiritual growth? When might it not be part of His plan?

4. If God were to allow Satan to move in on you or someone you love as He allowed him to do with Job, how would you respond? Would God have a fight on His hands? Which of Job's four responses—worship, humility, silence, and acceptance—would be difficult for you to apply? Why?

5. Spend some time reading and discussing these New Testament passages. What truths surface regarding the role of suffering in the life of faith? How can these insights be applied to Christians today? Discuss your thoughts.

> John 9:1–3
> 2 Timothy 1:7–10
> 1 Peter 4:16–19
> Romans 5:3
> Hebrews 2:10
> Philippians 1:29; 3:10
> James 1:2–3

Chapter 3

HOW TO SAY "NO"
WHEN LUST SAYS "YES"

Genesis 39

Moral failure usually doesn't just happen.

Occasionally, a temptation may broadside us. But more often, a series of slow, unattended leaks seeping from the lining of our character eventually weakens us to the point of a blowout. The next thing we know, frayed pieces of our once godly character lie strewn across the landscape for all to see.

Sadly, in recent decades the unbelieving world has stumbled over the shameful debris left by Christians whose desires got the better of them. Daily headlines chronicle the grim details of individual after individual, church after church, ministry after ministry reduced to heaps of scrap metal by single acts of moral or ethical indiscretion.

It doesn't have to end so tragically, though. God's Word tells us that there are happy endings, that many have withstood the lure of lust and escaped its destruction, and that you and I have real hope in this relentless battle between Spirit and flesh!

One story from the life of Joseph provides us with such good news. Joseph recognized the danger signs and adjusted his course long before he reached the point of no return. Let's take a look at Genesis 39 and watch how he avoided moral disaster by saying no to lust and swerving away from its ruinous path.

The Historical Situation

How did Joseph wind up in a position of having to say no to lust? The Bible makes clear that it wasn't by his own doing. Let's trace Joseph's life to see how he ended up where he did.

Joseph's ten older brothers despised him passionately. This hatred was stirred by their father's favoritism and also by Joseph's naïve use of a gift to foresee the future in dreams (see Gen. 37:2–11). In anger, his brothers sold him to a caravan of Ishmaelites en route to Egypt, who then sold him to Potiphar, an Egyptian officer (vv. 18–36). Potiphar was a wealthy man of high political rank who viewed Joseph as merely investment property. But God didn't view Joseph that way at all:

> The Lord was with Joseph, so he became a successful man. And he was in the house of his master, the Egyptian. (39:2)

The Lord's blessing on Joseph's life, coupled with his proven integrity, jettisoned him to a place of trust and prominence:

> Now his master saw that the Lord was with him and how the Lord caused all that he did to prosper in his hand. So Joseph found favor in his sight and became his personal servant; and he made him overseer over his house, and all that he owned he put in his charge. It came about that from the time he made him overseer in his house and over all that he owned, the Lord blessed the Egyptian's house on account of Joseph; thus the Lord's blessing was upon all that he owned, in the house and in the field. So he left everything he owned in Joseph's charge; and with him there he did not concern himself with anything except the food which he ate.[1] (vv. 3–6a)

The Sensual Temptation

Having baited us to follow this compelling tale by making us feel good about Joseph's fate, the narrator sets the hook with a tantalizing aside: "Now Joseph was handsome in form and appearance" (v. 6b).

---

1. The underlying theme of the Genesis-Exodus narrative is in full view in Joseph's story. As Ronald Youngblood notes: "In his generation, he [Joseph], more than any other, represented Israel—as a people who struggled with God and with men and overcame . . . and as a source of blessing to the nations. . . . The story of God's dealings with the patriarchs foreshadows the subsequent Biblical account of God's purpose with Israel. It begins with the election and calling out of Abram from the post-Babel nations and ends with Israel in Egypt (in the person of Joseph) preserving the life of the nations. . . . So God would deliver Israel out of the nations (the exodus), eventually to send them on a mission of life to the nations." Note on Genesis 37:2 in *The NIV Study Bible,* ed. Kenneth L. Barker (Grand Rapids, Mich.: Zondervan Bible Publishers, 1985), p. 62. John H. Sailhamer adds that Joseph's story isn't "a story of the success of Joseph; rather, it is a story of God's faithfulness to his promises." "Genesis," *The Zondervan NIV Bible Commentary,* ed. Kenneth L. Barker and John R. Kohlenberger III (Grand Rapids, Mich.: Zondervan Publishing House, 1994), vol. 1, p. 48.

While Potiphar rested confidently in Joseph's remarkable reliability, his wife feasted her eyes on his well-built physique:

> It came about after these events that his master's wife looked with desire at Joseph, and she said, "Lie with me." (v. 7)

Joseph immediately said no, trying first to appeal to her reason and then to her conscience:

> But he refused and said to his master's wife, "Behold, with me here, my master does not concern himself with anything in the house, and he has put all that he owns in my charge. There is no one greater in this house than I, and he has withheld nothing from me except you, because you are his wife. How then could I do this great evil and sin against God?" (vv. 8–9)

But the woman's lust was unabated. She scoffed at preserving the sanctity of her marriage or the delicate trust forged between Joseph and her husband. She only wanted to satiate her appetite for sexual pleasure—and Joseph's honorable reproach was too bitter a pill for her to swallow.

Let's pause for a moment to clarify some specifics in Joseph's situation. First, he faced a difficult dilemma. The very place in which he lived and worked, Potiphar's household, brought him face-to-face with Potiphar's wife's seductive temptations. Second, her advances must have flattered Joseph's ego and aroused his desire. He was only human, after all. Third, the temptation was constant. Day after day, she pursued young Joseph, hoping his resolve would wear thin (v. 10). Fourth, she waited until she and Joseph were alone to proposition him, free from the fear of detection (v. 11).

All this only heightened Joseph's vulnerability. Undoubtedly, as a young man, his hormones were revving up his desire to succumb. *Nobody's going to know. Her husband's gone, the servants aren't around, she's willing, so what would it hurt? Everybody does it!*

But Joseph reined in his sexual urges and exercised self-control. Potiphar's wife, however, did not:

> She caught him by his garment, saying, "Lie with me!" And he left his garment in her hand and fled, and went outside. (v. 12)

Joseph ran—which is just what the New Testament tells us to do in dealing with sexual temptation (see 1 Cor. 6:18 and 2 Tim. 2:22). Some things we're to stand and resist. But when it comes to sexual lust, we should remove ourselves from the situation of temptation as quickly as we can!

Personal Ramifications

There's an old saying:

> "Heaven has no rage like love to hatred turned,
> Nor hell a fury like a woman scorned."[2]

Potiphar's wife's unquenched lust suddenly blazed into a fury of revenge:

> When she saw that he had left his garment in her hand and had fled outside, she called to the men of her household and said to them, "See, he has brought in a Hebrew to us to make sport of us; he came in to lie with me, and I screamed. When he heard that I raised my voice and screamed, he left his garment beside me and fled and went outside." So she left his garment beside her until his master came home. Then she spoke to him with these words, "The Hebrew slave, whom you brought to us, came in to me to make sport of me; and as I raised my voice and screamed, he left his garment beside me and fled outside."
>
> Now when his master heard the words of his wife, which she spoke to him saying, "This is what your slave did to me," his anger burned. So Joseph's master took him and put him into the jail, the place where the king's prisoners were confined; and he was there in the jail. (Gen. 39:13–20)

Joseph didn't hear angels laud him for resisting the siren's call. What he heard instead was a woman's lie—a vengeful rant that hurled him headlong from the heights of privilege to the dungeons of obscurity.[3]

2. William Congreve, as quoted by John Bartlett in *Familiar Quotations*, 15th ed., rev. and enl., ed. Emily Morison Beck (Boston, Mass.: Little, Brown and Co., 1980), p. 324.

3. Even though Joseph was imprisoned as a common criminal, in the eyes of the Lord he was a faithful servant, a model of 1 Peter 2:20: "For what credit is there if, when you sin and are harshly treated, you endure it with patience? But if when you do what is right and suffer for it you patiently endure it, this finds favor with God." Because of the Lord's blessing, Joseph found favor with the chief jailer. To see what happened next, read Genesis 39:21–23.

Practical Applications for Christians

What lessons can we take into our lives from Joseph's example? At least four important principles come to mind that will help us say no when lust says yes.

First: *We must not be weakened by our situation.* Several aspects of Joseph's position could have undercut his resolve to say no to lust: he was trusted and secure in his job, extremely good-looking and popular, and in a position of authority and autonomy. It's easy to abuse trust, trade on our charm, and allow our freedom to become an occasion to sin, isn't it? Our temporal situation can easily obscure eternal realities, so we need to constantly remind ourselves that our our good gifts come from God and that we are accountable to Him.

Second: *We must not be deceived by persuasion.* Potiphar's wife's attempts to seduce Joseph were bold, flattering, calculating, and tantalizing. No doubt her verbal enticements were extremely tempting to Joseph. We don't know exactly what her persuasive words were back then, but we hear some false messages today as well: "Your wife doesn't love you like she should," "By doing this, you will prove you really love me," "No one will ever find out—we're perfectly safe," or "Look, we're going to be married in a few months, so what does it matter?" We need to train our ears to recognize the deceit in these destructive messages.

Third: *We must not be gentle with our emotions.* Joseph refused, and Joseph fled. He didn't give himself any time to think about how he was feeling. Temptation needs to be dealt with swiftly. F. B. Meyer exhorts us to "resist the first tiny rill of temptation, lest it widen a breach big enough to admit the ocean. Remember that no temptation can master you unless you admit it *within.*"[4]

Fourth: *We must not be confused by the immediate results.* We shouldn't be surprised if, like Joseph, our "Mrs. Potiphars" keep coming back to tempt us after we've said no. Resisting temptation once doesn't banish the threat forever. Lust is a resilient foe that will attack the next day—or even the next minute. So be on guard.

Joseph knew that God's blessing for obedience, though certain, was often deferred. In fact, the Lord used each of Joseph's triumphs and trials to prepare him for a greater task—ruling the entire nation of Egypt with honor!

---

4. F. B. Meyer, *Joseph: Beloved—Hated—Exalted* (Fort Washington, Pa.: Christian Literature Crusade, n.d.), p. 34.

That's how God works. He promises to honor our faithfulness—even if that means waiting for heaven's sure rewards.

Living Insights

Wherever God calls us to serve Him, in a place of prominence like Joseph or in the routine of common living, the Devil has his traps—and they're littered with the wreckage of those who either blindly rushed into a situation of temptation or stubbornly ignored the warning signs.

Victory over lust is rooted in our willingness to trust God's way as the best way. Since Eden, the Enemy has tried to convince us otherwise—tricking us into believing that *we* hold the keys to personal happiness and fulfillment, not God. Sin at any level is selling out to that lie, plain and simple.

But Joseph simply couldn't be bought. His forefathers Isaac and Jacob were cloaked with the mantle of godliness, but limped through history, sometimes trusting God, but more often giving in to their own desires. However, Joseph demonstrated wholehearted allegiance to God's program. And that allegiance included turning his back on lust's sensual invitation.

We as Christians are faced with similar decisions almost every day. In each encounter—whether it be a stubborn habit, an opportunity to go deeper in debt, or an invitation to pursue an inappropriate relationship—our faith in God's promises is tested. Passing that test involves rigorous spiritual discipline and humble submission to the Holy Spirit.

God's game plan for Christians is made plain in the Bible. His commands are not arbitrary. They are given for our good and His glory. Holiness is the by-product of a life surrendered in faith to Jesus Christ and wholeheartedly committed to His Word.

Thankfully, Jesus Christ provides the power for us to wage war against lust's menacing attacks. Romans contains our battle cry:

> For the law of the Spirit of life in Christ Jesus has set you free from the law of sin and of death. For what the Law could not do, weak as it was through the flesh, God did: sending His own Son in the likeness of sinful flesh and as an offering for sin, He condemned sin in the flesh, so that the requirement

of the Law might be fulfilled in us, who do not walk according to the flesh but according to the Spirit. . . . For the mind set on the flesh is death, but the mind set on the Spirit is life and peace. (vv. 2–4, 6)

Our decision to live by the Spirit or to fulfill the lusts of the flesh is a choice between blessing and misery. Are you really prepared to risk everything for a few moments of sensual pleasure? Jesus emphasized the extreme importance of resisting sin in Matthew chapter 18:

"If your eye causes you to stumble, pluck it out and throw it from you. It is better for you to enter life with one eye, than to have two eyes and be cast into the fiery hell." (v. 9)

Let that sink in. . . . It's always better to obey God and run from sin than to pick up the pieces of a broken life. Follow Joseph's example and say no to lust!

 ## Questions for Group Discussion

1. Clearly, a significant lesson to be learned from Joseph's temptation story is the importance of resisting lust's allure. Do you think that was God's only purpose for including this story in Genesis? How does Joseph being in Egypt relate to the promises made to Abraham in Genesis 12:1–3?

2. Why do you think God waits to fulfill His promise to bless our obedience? Share a time when you felt you upheld your end of the bargain but waited indefinitely for God to respond with His blessing.

3. What are some common pitfalls of temptation that Christians face today? Why do you think sexual immorality has become so prevalent among believers? How do you explain the severity with which Jesus and the apostles dealt with issues of sexual temptation? How does the book of Romans, especially chapters 7–8, provide hope for our battles between the Spirit and the flesh?

4. What is your concept of personal holiness? To what degree does it have to do with moral purity? What other aspects of holiness might be included in the Lord's concern?

Chapter 4

CULTIVATING OUR MARRIAGE WITH CHRIST

Psalm 51

This psalm isn't for the carefree Christian who is enjoying a close relationship with the Father. On the contrary, Psalm 51 is a cry for restoration.

David's straying from God left him exposed to the callous elements of sin's wintry night. Following a long drift from the Lord, David stood numbed by a blizzard of despair. He was broken and alone. His last drop of spiritual vitality had been frozen solid by frigid gusts of fear and shame. He didn't need a cold lecture . . . he longed for the thawing embrace of God's mercy.

Psalm 51 is a lyric reflection on God's plan of restoration for David, Israel's wayward king. Like David, all of us at times find ourselves left out in the cold by sin. Our wrong choices leave us in need of a word from heaven and desperate for a path that leads us back to God.

A Relationship on the Rocks

The Scriptures frequently describe the relationship between God and His people as a marriage. The New Testament teaches that tying the knot of faith immediately weds us to Christ by "the Holy Spirit of promise, who is given as a pledge" (Eph. 1:13b–14a). We are Christ's bride (see 2 Cor. 11:2; Eph. 5:22–23).

Old Testament writers also used this analogy, but often in the context of a marriage that's on the rocks. Many times the words "played the harlot" or "unfaithful" are used to characterize those who forsook God to worship pagan idols (see Judg. 8:27, 33; Josh. 22:16). The message is clear: spiritual adultery results in a divorce between our theology and our behavior.

Is it possible to mend a broken relationship with the Lord— no matter how unfaithful we've been? David says yes . . . and Psalm 51 shows us the steps that lead to restoration.

Claim God's Grace

Though David wandered far from God's favor, he could not venture beyond the limits of His grace. Ultimately, the prophet Nathan's penetrating words pierced David's sin-calloused heart, releasing an impassioned appeal for grace:[1]

> Be gracious to me, O God, according to Your
> lovingkindness;
> According to the greatness of Your compassion
> blot out my transgressions. (v. 1)

David recognized his need for *correction*. He slumped under the weight of his guilt, knowing that if God meted out justice, he would deserve death on the spot. So he reached for his only hope of forgiveness—God's grace. What constitutes this grace? A unique blend of God's lovingkindness and His great compassion (v. 1). Psalm 103:12 shows the vast extent of God's gracious forgiveness:

> As far as the east is from the west,
> So far has He removed our transgressions from us.

Have you ever tried going west until you found east? It's impossible! No matter how far west you go, you can always go farther. When God forgives us, He places an infinite distance between our sin and ourselves. We frequently remind ourselves of past failures, but God removes them permanently. He buries them in the depths of the sea (Mic. 7:19).

That's grace.

Confess Your Sins

Appealing to God's grace, David humbly confessed his sins to the Lord (Ps. 51:1–4). From his stirring confession, we may glean three helpful principles to apply when laying out our sins before the Lord.

---

1. This psalm's superscription connects David's prayer with his adultery with Bathsheba and his subsequent murder of her husband, Uriah. Commentator Willem A. VanGemeren notes that "the lament form of the psalm suitably fits the spirit of contrition and prayer for restoration. Gone are the questions. What remains is a soul deeply aware of sin, of having offended God, and of its desperate need of God's grace." "Psalms," in *The Expositor's Bible Commentary*, ed. Frank E. Gaebelein (Grand Rapids, Mich.: Zondervan Publishing House, 1991), vol. 5, p. 378.

Realize Their Seriousness

David didn't take his sins lightly. In verse 1 of Psalm 51, he called them "my transgressions." In verse 2, he prayed, "Wash me thoroughly from my iniquity/And cleanse me from my sin." He also expressed the nature of his sin in three ways. First, he portrayed his sin as a crime and asked for pardon: "Be gracious" (v. 1a). Second, he considered it a debt, asking God to "blot [it] out" (v. 1b). Third, he described it as a stain, asking God to "wash me thoroughly" (v. 2).

Accept Full Responsibility

David shouldered full responsibility for his sin. He didn't make excuses, concoct elaborate rationalizations, or attempt to shift the blame. He simply admitted the truth:

> For I know my transgressions,
> And my sin is ever before me.
> Against You, You only, I have sinned
> And done what is evil in Your sight,
> So that You are justified when You speak
> And blameless when You judge. (vv. 3–4)

Acknowledge Their Root

David recognized that God was just, holy, and blameless. He also acknowledged that his own nature was marred from the start, that corruption from Adam's fall was his lot from birth:

> Behold, I was brought forth in iniquity,
> And in sin my mother conceived me. (v. 5)

As Derek Kidner observes, David's sin "was no freak event: it was in character. . . . [His sins] are his own . . . the very element he lives in."[2] By pointing to his sin nature, David wasn't excusing himself, saying, "That's just the way I am," or blaming his parents. Instead, he was acknowledging the vast gulf that separated him from his Lord. David's transgressions went beyond the acts of committing adultery with Bathsheba and murdering her husband, Uriah (see 2 Sam. 11). David was, by nature, contaminated by sin; it came as naturally to him (and to all of us) as breathing.

---

2. Derek Kidner, *Psalms 1–72: An Introduction and Commentary on Books I and II of the Psalms*, Tyndale Old Testament Commentaries Series (Downers Grove, Ill.: InterVarsity Press, 1973), pp. 190–91.

But sin is as foreign to God as dark is to light, as false is to true. For at least nine months, David had lived a lie to conceal his sins (2 Sam. 11:5, 26–27). Perhaps this was in his mind as he wrote the next lines of his psalm:

> Behold, You desire truth in the innermost being,
> And in the hidden part You will make me know
> wisdom. (Ps. 51:6)

"Truth" is more than just telling accurate facts. It's being reliable and trustworthy,[3] being real and having integrity.[4] This is what God desires, and this is what David and the rest of us so often lack. Mercifully, however, the Lord doesn't turn us away or reject us because of our imperfection. As David knew, what the Lord desires, He helps form—He would teach David the way of wisdom.

In the next verses, David asked the Lord to do the things he could not do for himself:

> Purify me with hyssop,[5] and I shall be clean;
> Wash me, and I shall be whiter than snow.
> Make me to hear joy and gladness,
> Let the bones which You have broken rejoice.
> Hide Your face from my sins
> And blot out all my iniquities. (vv. 7–9)

In essence, David asked God to "de-sin" him.[6] Only the Lord could take his scarlet sinfulness and make his soul white as snow (see Isa. 1:18). Only the Lord could restore his emotional and physical health and renew his spirit with joy (see Prov. 3:8; Neh. 8:10). Only the Lord could blot out the record of David's sins, granting His child complete forgiveness (see Isa. 43:25; Mic. 7:18). As God told Jeremiah concerning His wayward people:

---

3. Walter Brueggemann, *The Message of the Psalms: A Theological Commentary*, Augsburg Old Testament Studies Series (Minneapolis, Minn.: Augsburg Publishing House, 1984), p. 100.

4. G. A. F. Knight, *Psalms*, vol. 1, The Daily Study Bible Series (Philadelphia, Pa.: Westminster Press, 1982), p. 244.

5. Hyssop was "the sprinkling instrument effecting propitiation of divine wrath (Ex. 12:12, 22, 23), ending exclusion and alienation (Lev. 14:6), purifying from defilement (Num. 19:16–19)." J. A. Motyer, "The Psalms," in *New Bible Commentary: 21st Century Edition*, 4th ed., rev., ed. D. A. Carson, R. T. France, J. A. Motyer, and G. J. Wenham (Downers Grove, Ill.: InterVarsity Press, 1994), p. 519.

6. Kidner, *Psalms 1–72*, p. 191; Motyer, "The Psalms," p. 519.

"I will forgive their iniquity, and their sin I will remember no more." (Jer. 31:34b)

Trusting the Lord to remove from him all that was wrong, David next asked God to remake him according to all that was right.

Construct New Patterns

In verses 10–12 of Psalm 51, David shifted his focus from *correction* to *construction*—beginning new patterns of living.

Renew Me!

> Create in me a clean heart, O God,
> And renew a steadfast spirit within me. (v. 10)

David longed to return to a lifestyle of godliness, so he asked God to create a "clean heart," or new beginning, for him. G. A. F. Knight explains that the Hebrew verb *create* "is one that is used of God only, never of man's work; it is the verb we find at Gen. 1:1. The miracle is, then, that forgiveness is in fact *re*-creation!"[7]

David also asked God to renew in him a *steadfast spirit*—a firmness of purpose that would keep him from wandering away from God, and an appetite for holiness that would find sin's once-alluring delicacies completely distasteful.

David's passionate plea for renewal, however, was tempered by two haunting fears: rejection by God and the removal of the Holy Spirit's presence from his life:

> Do not cast me away from Your presence
> And do not take Your Holy Spirit from me. (v. 11)

David feared he had finally crossed the line and was now in danger of losing the Spirit's presence permanently.[8] No doubt the fiery images of Saul's demise still burned in his mind (see 1 Sam. 16:14). Only the assurance of the Lord's salvation could relieve David's anxiety. And that's what David prayed for next.

---

7. Knight, *Psalms*, p. 244.

8. This fear is unjustified for Christians—we have received the full assurance of forgiveness through the revelation of Jesus Christ; the gift of the Holy Spirit is irrevocable. However, as John F. Walvoord explains, the Spirit "may be hindered in His ministry by sin" (see also 1 Thess. 5:19). *The Holy Spirit: A Comprehensive Study of the Person and Work of the Holy Spirit* (1965; reprint, Grand Rapids, Mich.: Zondervan Publishing House, 1991), p. 72.

Restore Me!

First David asked for a steadfast, constant spirit (v. 10), then for the life-giving power of the Holy Spirit (v. 11), and now he prayed for an eager, willing spirit that would delight to do God's will:[9]

> Restore to me the joy of Your salvation,
> And sustain me with a willing spirit. (v. 12)

Left unchanged, David knew he'd wander back down the same slippery slope to sin. What he needed was a transforming joy brought on by glad submission to God that would hold greater sway over his darker instincts. David knew that lasting fulfillment would only come from knowing God intimately and submitting to Him willingly.

Communicate Your Change

Once he had claimed God's grace, confessed his transgressions, and asked God for new life patterns, what was David's next step? He wanted to share God's mercy with others.

Teach Sinners

> Then I will teach transgressors Your ways,
> And sinners will be converted to You. (v. 13)

David knew the way of transgressors because he *was* one. He knew their heartaches and fears. But he also knew that the Lord could provide love and restoration to sinners and bring them back into loving fellowship with Him.

Praise God

David then expressed his gratitude for God's merciful grace through praise:

> Deliver me from bloodguiltiness, O God, the God
>   of my salvation;
> Then my tongue will joyfully sing of Your
>   righteousness.
> O Lord, open my lips,

---

9. Notice that in verses 10–12, "three times there is reference to 'spirit/wind'. . . . The first is a request for a new spirit (compare Ezek. 36:26), a chance to begin again. The latter two are a recognition that the 'wind' to live is a gift from God." Brueggemann, *The Message of the Psalms*, p. 100.

That my mouth may declare Your praise.
For You do not delight in sacrifice, otherwise I would
give it;
You are not pleased with burnt offering;
The sacrifices of God are a broken spirit;
A broken and contrite heart, O God, You will not
despise. (vv. 14–17)

Only when God Himself released David from the crushing guilt of his sin could the grieved king's spirit lift in praise. As Derek Kidner observes, "The prayer *open thou my lips* is no mere formula but the cry of one whose conscience has shamed him into silence."[10] No animal sacrifice could atone for what David had done,[11] and God wouldn't have wanted that anyway—not without the sacrifices of humility and brokenness coming first (see Isa. 29:13a; 57:15b).

God wants our hearts more than anything else, and David made this truth sparkling clear in his psalm.

Pray for God's Blessing

As God's appointed king, David knew that his decisions and actions affected the nation, not just himself and those directly involved in his transgressions. So as he closed his psalm, he prayed for God's blessing on Israel and for the nation's strength and security:

By Your favor do good to Zion;
Build the walls of Jerusalem.
Then You will delight in righteous sacrifices,
In burnt offering and whole burnt offering;
Then young bulls will be offered on Your altar.[12]
(Ps. 51:18–19)

10. Kidner, *Psalms 1–72*, p. 193.

11. As J. A. Motyer reminds us, the "sins of adultery . . . and murder . . . were not covered by sacrificial provision" in the Mosaic Law. "The Psalms," p. 518.

12. Many commentators (Brueggemann, Kidner, Knight, VanGemeren) suggest that verses 18–19 were added to this psalm by the post-exilic community. As G.A.F. Knight explains, "Though they had come back home to Jerusalem physically some years earlier, . . . only now with the dedication of the temple did there take place the end of their separation from God in a spiritual sense. Consequently, the whole sacrificial system that atoned for the sins of Israel could now be re-instituted, and Israel could live once again as the Holy People in continually renewed fellowship with the Holy God." *Psalms*, p. 248.

Despite the far-reaching effects of our sins, God's lovingkindness, compassion, and forgiveness reach even farther. Through the perfect atoning sacrifice of His Son, Jesus Christ, He lifts us up, frees us from guilt's stranglehold, sets us on the path of life, and grants us a glorious new beginning!

If you've been feeling estranged from the Lover of your soul because of some sin in your life, take your cue from David. As his psalm shows us, nothing can separate a humble and contrite sinner from the love of God (compare Rom. 8:31–39). *Nothing*. That's grace—a grace that wants reconciliation even more than we do!

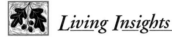 *Living Insights*

Have you ever wondered what forgiveness *sounds* like? Psalm 51 says forgiveness sounds like *singing*! David said he would hear gladness and joy as a result of God's gracious forgiveness.

Perhaps you've been on a long drift away from the Lord and, like David, you are stumbling under the weight of guilt. Your song is gone. The people closest to you have stopped singing, too. Joy and gladness have escaped through the cracks in your soul and haven't been heard in your home in weeks—maybe months—perhaps even years.

If you know Christ as your Savior, He has provided a way for you to be restored. And that's by simply coming to Him as David did: humbly . . . with a broken heart . . . confessing sin. Jesus is a merciful Savior who longs to have intimate fellowship with you and to lavish His love on you. Consider this New Testament truth:

> If we confess our sins, He is faithful and righteous to forgive us our sins and to cleanse us from all unrighteousness. (1 John 1:9)

That's Psalm 51, New Testament style! Jesus wants to cleanse you from your sin today. He desires to give you a fresh start and a clean slate. He wants you to start *singing* again.

On the next page, use the outline of Psalm 51 to construct your prayer of confession to the Lord. Or simply close this book and call out to Him for mercy. He'll be there . . . He promises.

My Personal Prayer of Confession

1. *Claim God's grace.* Make this request of God: "Be gracious to me, O God, according to Your lovingkindness, forgive me for my sin."

_____

_____

_____

_____

2. *Confess your sins.* Address each by name, taking full responsibility for them.

_____

_____

_____

_____

3. *Construct new patterns.* In your own words, ask the Lord for renewal and restoration.

_____

_____

_____

_____

4. *Communicate your change.* Write down some ways you can communicate God's grace to others who may be desperately in need of it.

_____

_____

_____

_____

Now take some time to prayerfully ask the Lord to help those who may have been injured by your sinful actions. They, too, can experience His grace and love and start down the path of renewal and restoration. Remember, healing takes time. So be patient with yourself, with others, and especially with the Lord.

The singing you hear in the distance is joy on its way back to your soul!

 *Questions for Group Discussion*

1. Based on what we've studied in this chapter, what essential attitudes must Christians express to be restored to a right relationship with Christ? How did David demonstrate these attitudes in his prayer? What was his mind-set toward God's justice?

2. Read back through Psalm 51 and discuss the multitude of ways David described the character of God. What are some of His attributes? How does having a correct view of God help us grasp the seriousness of sin?

3. Verses 5–9 are rich in imagery. What are some of the most vivid images David used, and how do they help us understand the meaning of this psalm? Ultimately, what did David want from the Lord?

4. Worship is another major theme in this psalm. In what ways does sin hinder our worship of the Savior? How does brokenness contribute to genuine Christian worship? What sorts of worshipful expressions sprang from David's forgiveness (see vv. 14–17)?

5. Spend some time reading 1 John 1:8–2:2 together. How does this New Testament passage relate to our study of Psalm 51? How is Christ our advocate? What impact does having a righteous advocate have on our daily discipline of confessing sins?

Chapter 5

HOW TO DISCERN
WITHOUT JUDGING

1 Samuel 16:1–13

Let's play "Who Wants to Be a Billionaire?"!

Okay. You're going for one billion dollars! Are you ready? Here's the question: "When is it appropriate for Christians to judge?"

a. When others are different from us.

b. When a serious sin has taken place.

c. When seeking new employees.

d. Never. Judging is always sin!

Time ticks away. You muse: "We've discussed this so many times in our small group Bible study. And nobody seems to know. Judging is wrong most of the time, but it seems the Bible does say it's okay in certain situations."

Long pause. You feel the sweat bead across your furrowed brow and drip down the side of your face.

The world waits silently.

Should I use a lifeline? you wonder, fidgeting. *But who would know? Who could I call? Maybe I should ask the audience . . . but what if there's no consensus?*

What's my final answer?

Ever felt that sort of pressure when trying to answer a tough question about your faith? Most of us have. The Christian life is full of challenging queries, and often we feel caught off guard and pressured for a response.

Thankfully, we have a "final answer"—using the lifeline of God's Word, the Bible. The Scriptures show us *how* and *when* we are to judge in a way that honors people and pleases the Lord.

In fact, the Bible teaches that every mature believer possesses the important ability to practice *discernment.* And as we watch the unfolding of a poignant Old Testament story, we'll begin to see how we, too, can cultivate this indispensable quality of authentic Christianity.

A Prophet, a Family, and an Unlikely King

The preface to our story concerns Saul, a king who had little discernment regarding spiritual things. Rather than obeying the Lord's command completely, he fulfilled part of it and adapted the rest to suit his own preferences. The result? God dethroned him. The prophet Samuel told Saul: "The Lord has torn the kingdom of Israel from you today and has given it to your neighbor, *who is better than you*" (1 Sam. 15:28, emphasis added).

It was a stinging pronouncement, and a little while after delivering it, Samuel left Saul, never to see him again. God had dispatched Samuel to select a new king—a man with a better heart than Saul—from the house of Jesse and to anoint him with the refreshing oil of His good favor.

Samuel's Instructions

Now the Lord said to Samuel, "How long will you grieve over Saul, since I have rejected him from being king over Israel? Fill your horn with oil and go; I will send you to Jesse the Bethlehemite, for I have selected a king for Myself among his sons." But Samuel said, "How can I go? When Saul hears of it, he will kill me." And the Lord said, "Take a heifer with you and say, 'I have come to sacrifice to the Lord.' You shall invite Jesse to the sacrifice, and I will show you what you shall do; and you shall anoint for Me the one whom I designate to you." (16:1–3)

Even Samuel, Israel's most respected man, was afraid of the volatile Saul. So the Lord showed him how to safely carry out His orders. Since God had called Samuel to be a priest, prophet, and judge, he traveled to various communities to settle disputes, confront sins, and offer sacrifices. The sacrifice with Jesse and his family, then, would look like an ordinary part of his duties, and Saul would have no reason to suspect anything different.

So Samuel did what the Lord said, and came to Bethlehem. And the elders of the city came trembling to meet him and said, "Do you come in peace?" He said, "In peace; I have come to sacrifice to the Lord. Consecrate yourselves and come with me to the sacrifice." He also consecrated Jesse and his sons

41

and invited them to the sacrifice. (vv. 4–5)

The elders of Bethlehem probably feared that Samuel had come to pronounce God's judgment on them. Instead, he graciously invited them to worship the Lord in preparation for one of history's most thrilling events—the anointing of God's shepherd-king.

Samuel's Dilemma

Israel's esteemed prophet surveyed each of Jesse's sons, with his gaze initially resting on Jesse's eldest son, Eliab:

> When they entered, he looked at Eliab and thought, "Surely the Lord's anointed is before Him." (v. 6)

Apparently, Eliab was tall and handsome, and Samuel hastily concluded that he must be God's choice. The Lord, however, had a much different perspective:

> But the Lord said to Samuel, "Do not look at his appearance or at the height of his stature, because I have rejected him; for God sees not as man sees, for man looks at the outward appearance, but the Lord looks at the heart." (v. 7)

A cursory glance at outward appearances offers little insight into a person's character. Only the Spirit's gaze penetrates deeply enough to reveal the true nature of our hearts. Samuel mistakenly made his judgment based on Eliab's looks. God, on the other hand, discerned that Eliab's character did not match his strong facade. So He rejected him as a candidate for king.

Samuel proceeded to the next son:

> Then Jesse called Abinadab and made him pass before Samuel. And he said, "The Lord has not chosen this one either." (v. 8)

And the next one:

> Next Jesse made Shammah pass by. And he said, "The Lord has not chosen this one either." (v. 9)

And Samuel looked over the one after him, and the next one after him, and the son after that:

> Thus Jesse made seven of his sons pass before Samuel.

But Samuel said to Jesse, "The Lord has not chosen these." (v. 10)

Samuel's Selection

Bewildered by this turn of events, Samuel asked Jesse if he had presented all of his sons. To his relief, Jesse had one more boy, his youngest, who remained in the field tending his father's flock (v. 11a). So Samuel told him:

> "Send and bring him; for we will not sit down until he comes here." So he sent and brought him in. Now he was ruddy, with beautiful eyes and handsome appearance.[1] (vv. 11b–12a)

Could he be the one? Samuel must have thought he *had* to be—they'd run out of sons! And sure enough, the Lord told him:

> "Arise, anoint him; for this is he." (v. 12b)

Samuel fixed his seasoned gaze firmly on Israel's next king—a young man whose only qualifying experience was leading and protecting his stubborn, woolly flock. Yet the prophet didn't hesitate to trust God's judgment of David's character. Instead, he gladly fulfilled the task God sent him to perform:

> Then Samuel took the horn of oil and anointed him in the midst of his brothers; and the Spirit of the Lord came mightily upon David from that day forward. And Samuel arose and went to Ramah. (1 Sam. 16:13)

How perfectly fitting that God chose a shepherd to lead Israel's sheep into the rich pastures of blessing (see Ps. 78:70–72)! David entered the story of the Bible in the least likely manner. Not unlike the Savior, he came as a humble servant, destined to rule Israel. David was anointed king, and God's Spirit guided and empowered him to accomplish the Lord's plans from that day forward.

---

1. The word *ruddy* means "reddish," probably referring to "healthy reddish skin." The Hebrews "found great beauty in a ruddy complexion." (See *The International Standard Bible Encyclopedia*, rev. ed., gen. ed. Geoffrey W. Bromiley [Grand Rapids, Mich.: William B. Eerdmans Publishing Co., 1988], vol. 4, p. 238.) David also had "beautiful eyes"—eyes that would prove more sensitive to the Lord and wisely discerning than those of his ill-fated predecessor, Saul.

Insights from Samuel's Experience

What would Samuel say to us today based on what he learned on that all-important day in Israel's history? Four important truths can be gleaned from his experience.

First, *mistakes are made when we judge quickly based on surface evidence.* With one look at Eliab, Samuel assumed that he was God's choice for king, but he couldn't have been more wrong. Snap judgments based on surface impressions often result in poor decisions. And those poor decisions usually turn into painful consequences and regrets. We need to slow down and take time to study a person's character and heart.

Second, *looking at the heart doesn't come naturally to us.* First Samuel 16:7 makes clear our tendency to judge on externals: "God sees not as man sees, for man looks at the outward appearance, but the Lord looks at the heart." We can change, or at least temper, our natural tendency when we yield to the Spirit's control. As we grow in our relationship with Christ, our new nature blossoms and prompts us to see more as God sees. That's the essence of discernment.

Third, *people we may consider insignificant are significant to God.* With God, there are no "little people." David, the youngest in his family, was overlooked by those closest to him (v. 11). How often do we do the same thing—with those who are younger, older, in a different financial situation, physically challenged, or less attractive? But we are *all* made in the image of God, never overlooked by Him, so we need to resist our natural bent toward discounting others. Jesus Himself reminds us that how we treat others is how we treat Him (see Matt. 25:40).

And fourth, *appearance matters to God.* Remember the first information given to us about David? Ironically, it's a description of his looks—"ruddy, with beautiful eyes and a handsome appearance" (v. 12). Now that is curious, since God was careful to teach Samuel a lesson about judging too hastily from outward appearances! But apparently, appearance *does* matter to God. He desires that we look our best and take care of the bodies He has given us (see 1 Cor. 6:19–20). David had both the character and the physical presence fitting for a king.

New Testament Insights and Guidelines on Judging

In addition to the lessons we've learned from Samuel, the New Testament has much to teach us about judging others. In Matthew

7:1, Jesus warns against self-righteously condemning others:

"Do not judge so that you will not be judged."

Jesus most likely had the Pharisees in mind when He said this. Throughout His Sermon on the Mount, He contrasts their ways with the ways of God's kingdom (Matt. 5–7). These religious leaders frequently burdened the people with self-exalting and hypocritical judgments. They were more often motivated by harsh criticism than genuine concern for others.

Rather than condoning judgmental ways, Jesus urges us to put ourselves in the other's place (7:2) and to honestly address the faults in ourselves before criticizing anyone else (vv. 3–5). "*All* have sinned," the apostle Paul later reminded us, "and fall short of the glory of God" (Rom. 3:23, emphasis added). Scripture is not promoting a "flabby indifference to moral wrong but recognition of solidarity in guilt."[2]

In fact, Hebrews 5:14 explains that God wants mature believers to exercise wise judgment:

> But solid food is for the mature, who because of
> practice have their senses trained to *discern* good and
> evil. (emphasis added)

The Greek term used here for *discern* is *diakrisis*, which is related to *krino*, the word Jesus used in Matthew 7 to mean "judge." Here the term "usually means 'discernment' or 'differentiation.'"[3] Christian maturity is marked by our ability to distinguish good from evil, right from wrong.

Apparently, the Hebrew believers were struggling with how to make sound moral choices. They needed to grow in their ability to choose what honored Christ, as well as in their skill at lovingly guiding others in His righteous ways (see Romans 14).

Let's consider some situations in which genuine biblical discernment is essential.

When prolonged involvement is being considered. Whether we're choosing a roommate, a close friend, a business partner, or a spouse, discernment is crucial. Decisions such as choosing a church, a new

2. Gerhard Kittel and Gerhard Friedrich, eds., *Theological Dictionary of the New Testament,* translated and abridged in one volume by Geoffrey W. Bromiley (1985; reprint, Grand Rapids, Mich.: William B. Eerdmans Publishing Co., 1992), p. 472.

3. Kittel and Friedrich, eds., *Theological Dictionary of the New Testament,* p. 474.

job, or some other ministry association also warrant a prayerful discernment process.

When fractures in the body of Christ need mending. Galatians 6:1 tells us to restore "in a spirit of gentleness" a fellow believer who has fallen into sin and to humbly watch our own tendency to succumb to temptation. And James 5:19–20 encourages us that one who turns another back to the Lord has performed a soul-saving work and "will cover a multitude of sins." In short, we are instructed to approach wayward Christians with soothing medicine, not clubs of condemnation! Compassionate discernment always honors the Lord and springs from a heart of love for our brothers and sisters in Christ.

When designating leaders. Unfortunately, ministry leadership elections often resemble political campaigns or popularity contests. Paul, however, cautioned his young apprentice Timothy to not choose leaders hastily, because if they fell into sin, he would share the responsibility (1 Tim. 5:22). Choosing leaders has nothing to do with expedience, popularity, or availability. Leadership selection has everything to do with wise discernment based on a candidate's character and commitment to Christ.

When distinguishing truth from error. Paul warned Timothy about those who cloud distinctions between correct doctrine and doctrine skewed by human manipulation (1 Tim. 6:3–5). John expressed the same pressing concern when he urged believers not to "believe every spirit, but test the spirits to see whether they are from God, because many false prophets have gone out into the world" (1 John 4:1). "We are no longer to be children," added Paul, "tossed here and there by . . . every wind of doctrine," but we are to grow and mature in the truth and love of Christ (Eph. 4:14–15).

Conclusion

So, with believers and nonbelievers watching, the spotlight burning into your eyes, and the clock ticking, what do you say? When and how is it appropriate for Christians to judge?

If you're not quite ready yet to give your final answer, you'll have an opportunity to dig more deeply into the lifeline of God's Word in the following Living Insights. Finding the right answer may not make you a billionaire, but you'll be rich in God's wisdom and grace!

Living Insights

How balanced are you when it comes to exercising spiritual discernment and godly judgment? Do you tend to be too soft, too tolerant, so you don't make waves? Or do you lean more toward holding rigid opinions that ossify your love for others? Take a moment to test yourself. For instance, how would you react if:

- a teenager with purple hair and a nose ring walked into your church worship service?

- a biracial couple visited your Sunday school class?

- a church member told you her teenage daughter was three months pregnant?

- in casual conversation, a woman in your Bible study group mentioned she was married to her third husband?

- you heard your pastor exhort you and the congregation to reach out to the homosexual community thriving only blocks away from the church?

- a list of nominated church leaders included an individual whom you knew to be an abusive father?

- you heard a Sunday school teacher consistently refer to the story of the Virgin Birth as a beautiful allegory?

These thorny scenarios are surprisingly common. How can believers discern an appropriate response to these and similar situations? We need the Scriptures as our guide and the Holy Spirit as our helper.

Take some time to look up and prayerfully read each of the following New Testament passages. As you do, jot down some notes regarding how they contribute to your understanding of judgment and discernment. Ask the Holy Spirit to impress on your mind and heart any areas you need to bring into balance. Jot down those thoughts as well. This may take some time, but you may be pleasantly surprised by how clearly the Lord speaks to you through His Word today!

Mark 2:15–17 _____

Luke 18:9–14 _____

_____

John 8:1–11 _____

_____

Romans 2:1–4 _____

_____

Romans 14:4, 10–13, 19 _____

_____

Romans 15:7 _____

_____

1 Corinthians 5:9–13 _____

_____

1 Corinthians 6:9b–11 _____

_____

Galatians 6:1–2 _____

_____

1 Timothy 1:5–7 _____

_____

2 Timothy 4:2–4 _____

_____

James 2:13 _____

_____

James 5:1–9 _____

_____

2 John 1:7–11 _____

_____

3 John 1:9–12 _____

_____

Jude 1:1–25 _____

_____

 ## *Questions for Group Discussion*

1. Now that you've interacted with the material in this chapter, discuss some of your reactions to what was presented. In what ways were your views on judging and discerning challenged or broadened?

2. Based on Scripture, how would you distinguish between a person who is wisely discerning and one who is judgmental? Give some real-life examples of both. In what ways are we as Christians to judge unbelievers, if at all?

3. Can you think of times when you were the victim of a judgmental attitude? Describe the circumstances. How did you feel?

4. Often when we reach out to new people, we tend to embrace those who share our standard of living or lifestyle and slight those who are different. Can you think of examples of how this might occur in a church setting? In what ways do Christians tend to judge people on appearances? Does this honor Christ?

5. What role does the Holy Spirit play in helping us achieve balance in this area of our Christian lives? Explain.

Chapter 6
A TRIUMPH OF TRUST
Genesis 22:1–14

Perhaps more than any other Old Testament character, Abraham repeatedly surfaces in the Bible as a model for authentic godly living. But how can an individual from antiquity teach us anything about practical Christianity today?

Like the steady beacon of a lighthouse which allows us to navigate through dark waters even when we can't see the rocks, Abraham's remarkable faith shines as a testimony to this truth: as believers, we are to walk by *faith* and not by *sight*.

Abraham's life demonstrates that it is our faith that pleases God most and ultimately secures us to Him. But that faith must be tested, forging our character and refining our trust to prepare us for the day when our faith will become sight.

Genesis 22 paints a portrait of Abraham as he faces his most severe test. At first, God's command that Abraham sacrifice his son shocks us, but gradually shock gives way to inspiration as we watch the aged patriarch overcome this towering trial with solemn, controlled obedience. Finally, we bow in humble adoration to worship a magnificent Lord who, moved by Abraham's triumphant trust, pours out His abundant blessings on him. And along the way, we gain valuable insights into how we, too, can prove our trust in the Lord and enjoy the blessings of obedience. Let's look at the challenging curriculum of personal crises that led up to Abraham's last agonizing test.

The School of Faith

A major theme in the Abraham narratives is that God tests His children. He allows these tests to vary in intensity in order to prove the genuineness of our faith (James 1: 2–4). God enrolled Abraham in the school of faith back in Genesis 12, guiding him through an intense learning period that climaxed with a rigorous final exam in chapter 22.

When Told to Leave Ur

The initial crisis came when God told Abraham to leave his home. At seventy-five, Abraham gathered his belongings and forsook his boyhood dwelling for a new and unfamiliar frontier—the land of God's promise. As everything he knew faded behind him, a vast uncertainty stretched before him. Nevertheless, Abraham trusted in God's promise to make his descendants a great nation through whom all people on earth would be blessed (Gen. 12:2–3). He said his goodbyes and willingly turned his back on Ur forever.

When Separating from Lot

Next, Abraham faced a family crisis when disagreement over grazing rights impelled him to separate from his nephew Lot (Gen. 13). The land simply could not sustain both families. So to avoid further strife, Abraham laid aside his personal needs and offered Lot the choicest land. Again, the seasoned patriarch trusted God and waited for Him to reveal the next step in His unfolding plan.

When Relinquishing Cherished Plans for Ishmael

Abraham had another son named Ishmael, who was born of Sarah's handmaiden, Hagar. The Lord had told Abraham and Sarah that they would have an heir, but because Sarah was barren, she suggested that Hagar have Abraham's child in her place. However, this was not God's plan. He had determined that the child of His promise would come from Abraham and Sarah, and no one else (17:15–16, 19–21). God insisted that Abraham relinquish any hope of realizing the promised blessing through Ishmael. Abraham's anguish is evident in his impassioned entreaty to the Lord:

> And Abraham said to God, "Oh that Ishmael might live before You!" But God said, "No, but Sarah your wife will bear you a son, and you shall call his name Isaac; and I will establish My covenant with him for an everlasting covenant for his descendants after him. (17:18–19)

Despite his deep love for Ishmael, Abraham determined to follow God's way and not his own.

A Faith Confirmed

Revelation of the Test

Unbelievably, in the fourth and final crisis, God commanded Abraham to take Isaac, his long-awaited son, and offer him as a sacrifice (Gen. 22).

Now it came about after these things, that God tested Abraham, and said to him, "Abraham!" And he said, "Here I am." He said, "Take now your son, your only son, whom you love, Isaac, and go to the land of Moriah, and offer him there as a burnt offering on one of the mountains of which I will tell you." (Gen. 22: 1–2)

The Hebrew word *nasah* means "tested." It suggests that this particular trial was of an extremely intense nature. This test would serve as Abraham's final exam in God's school of faith.

For us to appreciate fully the impact of this scene, we need to keep in mind that Abraham was over one hundred years old. He and Sarah waited years for the birth of Isaac. Through him, and him alone, God would fulfill His covenant (Gen. 15). We can only imagine Abraham's mental anguish as he envisioned a blazing altar, once reserved for bulls and goats, consuming his beloved Isaac and all the promises God offered through him![1]

Response of Abraham

Several aspects of Abraham's response help us understand characteristics of faithful obedience.

First, Abraham's response was *immediate*:

So Abraham rose early in the morning and saddled his donkey, and took two of his young men with him and Isaac his son; and he split wood for the burnt offering, and arose and went to the place of which God had told him. (Gen. 22:3)

No delays, no procrastination—only prompt compliance with God's command. One night was all that separated God's directive from Abraham's timely obedience.

Second, Abraham's response was *characterized by faith*:

On the third day Abraham raised his eyes and saw

---

1. The Hebrew word *olah*, used here to mean "offering," refers to a whole burnt offering, which would have included an animal's hooves, face, head, skin—*everything!* The entire animal would be consumed by fire, and this is just what God told Abraham to do with Isaac. An intense test indeed. For further discussion on this Hebrew word, see R. Laird Harris, Gleason L. Archer, Jr., and Bruce K. Waltke, eds., *Theological Wordbook of the Old Testament* (Chicago, Ill.: Moody Press, 1980), vol. 2, p. 666.

the place from a distance. Abraham said to his young men, "Stay here with the donkey, and I and the lad will go over there; and we will worship and *return to you*." (vv. 4–5, emphasis added)

As Mount Moriah loomed ominously on the horizon, Abraham remained focused on worshiping the Lord, trusting His ability even to raise Isaac from the dead if it came to that (see Heb. 11:17–19). Moreover, not one note of remorse, despondency, regret, or bitterness sounded from Abraham's lips in this entire symphony of faithful obedience.

Third, Abraham's response was *based on the character of God:*

Abraham took the wood of the burnt offering and laid it on Isaac his son, and he took in his hand the fire and the knife. So the two of them walked on together. Isaac spoke to Abraham his father and said, "My father!" And he said, "Here I am, my son." And he said, "Behold, the fire and the wood, but where is the lamb for the burnt offering?" Abraham said, "God will provide for Himself the lamb for the burnt offering, my son." So the two of them walked on together. (Gen. 22:6–8)

God had promised Abraham that his descendants and all the people of the earth would be blessed through Isaac. Even as he took the fire and the knife and led his son up the mountain, Abraham was silent and resolute. Isaac's stirring query prompted Abraham to finally break his silence and express a mind-boggling trust in the goodness of God. John Sailhamer describes Abraham's response this way:

Amid the anguish that the reader has read into Abraham's silence, there is now also a silent confidence in the Lord who will provide. Abraham's words should not be understood as merely an attempt to calm the curious Isaac; but in light of the fact that they anticipate the actual outcome of the narrative, they are to be read as a confident expression of his trust in God.[2]

2. John Sailhamer, *The Expositor's Bible Commentary* (Grand Rapids, Mich.: Zondervan Publishing House, 1990), vol. 2, pp. 168–69.

Abraham's compassionate, hope-filled answer reflected an unswerving trust in God's faithfulness. The obedient patriarch staked his entire future on the Lord's unchangeable nature.

Lastly, Abraham's response was *thorough and complete*. A brief review of the previous verses reveals Abraham's steady, deliberate preparation for his remarkable journey to Mount Moriah. He "saddled his donkey," "split wood," "built the altar," "arranged the wood," "bound his son Isaac," "laid him on the altar," "stretched out his hand," and "took the knife to slay his son" (Gen. 22:3–10). Abraham didn't shrink back from a single detail. And God rewarded his unflinching faith.

Reward of God

Abraham was prepared to plunge the knife deep into the bound body of Isaac when God finally intervened:

> But the angel of the Lord called to him from heaven and said, "Abraham, Abraham!" And he said, "Here I am." (v. 11)

How relieved Abraham must have been to hear a voice from heaven just then! Abraham listened intently for God's next instructions:

> He said, "Do not stretch out your hand against the lad, and do nothing to him; for now I know that you fear God, since you have not withheld your son, your only son, from Me." (v. 12)

According to the apostle James, Abraham proved the genuineness of his faith when he offered up his beloved Isaac on the altar (James 2: 21). God honored his faith by providing a fitting substitute for Isaac:

> Then Abraham raised his eyes and looked, and behold, behind him a ram caught in the thicket by his horns; and Abraham went and took the ram and offered him up for a burnt offering in the place of his son. Abraham called the name of that place The Lord Will Provide, as it is said to this day, "In the mount of the Lord it will be provided." (Gen. 22:13–14)

Overcome with joy and praise for the Lord's provision, Abraham named the site in honor of God's faithfulness. Then God rewarded

Abraham with a perpetual blessing that would impact generations to come:

> Then the angel of the Lord called to Abraham a second time from heaven, and said, "By Myself I have sworn, declares the Lord, because you have done this thing and have not withheld your son, your only son, indeed I will greatly bless you, and I will greatly multiply your seed as the stars of the heavens and as the sand which is on the seashore; and your seed shall possess the gate of their enemies. In your seed all the nations of the earth shall be blessed, because you have obeyed My voice." (vv. 15–18)

Faith Lessons We Can Learn

Abraham's story of proven and rewarded faith teaches us two important lessons about our relationship with the Lord.

First, *what we retain for ourselves, God asks us to release to Him.* God wants us to entrust to Him our children, our marriages, our careers, and our cherished dreams for the future—everything we hold dear. He is worthy of that trust.

Second, *God always honors faithful obedience.* He rewards those who believe His Word and seek Him with their hearts and lives (Heb. 11:6). But He cannot reward us if we stubbornly cling to the things of the world. He wants us to come to Him with empty hands so that He can fill them with His abundant blessings. That was true for Abraham, and it's true for you and me as well!

Often poetry expresses truth best:

> One by one He took them from me,
> All the things I valued most,
> Until I was empty-handed;
> Every glittering toy was lost,
>
> And I walked earth's highways, grieving,
> In my rags and poverty.
> Till I heard His voice inviting,
> "Lift your empty hands to Me!"
>
> So I held my hands toward Heaven,
> And He filled them with a store

Of His own transcendent riches
Till they could contain no more.

And at last I comprehended
With my stupid mind and dull,
That God COULD not pour His riches
Into hands already full![3]

Are you willing to empty your hands to Christ today?

 *Living Insights*
_____

Two-year-old Ben has a ritual he observes every morning. Before waddling down the hall to the family room, he gathers up his two blankets, his giant stuffed Winnie-the-Pooh and his fluffy stuffed lamb named Chop. Only then does he feel prepared to leave the safety of his warm, cozy bed to venture into the chilly uncertainty of another day.

As with most toddlers, Ben feels most secure when his little hands are full of soft, cuddly *things!*

Often, that is the way life unfolds for us as Christians. We clutch tightly to those things that give only a false sense of security and safety. But God wants us to trust Him—not soft cuddlies— especially in life's uncertainties.

As He did with Abraham, the Lord uses crises to test our willingness to let go and to trust Him to provide. What are some of the major crises the Lord has led you through?

_____

_____

_____

_____

_____

_____

3. Martha Snell Nicholson, "Treasures," in *Ivory Palaces* (Wilmington, Calif.: Martha Snell Nicholson, 1946), p. 67.

What things did you cling to then that kept you from fully trusting the Lord?

_____

_____

_____

_____

_____

_____

What lessons did you learn about God and His ability to provide in your time of crisis?

_____

_____

_____

_____

_____

Are you clutching anything in your hands today that hinders your faith in God's plan? What *things* do you hold tightly?

_____

_____

_____

_____

_____

Take some time to go to the Lord in prayer and ask Him to help you surrender those things to Him right now. It might help to open your hands, palms up, to Him as you pray.

And remember: as you let go, be assured of the fact the Lord has promised to pour back into your hands an abundant supply of His blessings!

Questions for Group Discussion

Undoubtedly, when Abraham offered his son, he faced the most difficult trial of his life. The story drips with pathos wrung from an anguished father's heart.

Read through the story in Genesis 22 again, this time putting yourself in Abraham's place and one of your children on the altar.

1. What doubts or questions may have come to Abraham's mind?

2. What do you think sustained Abraham during this crisis in his life (see Heb. 11:17–19)?

3. What role do crises play in our Christian lives (see James 1: 2–4)?

4. Read Romans 8:28–29. What observations can you make about God's plan?

5. What do you think the word *good* means in verse 28? How does that relate to faith?

Chapter 7

WHEN TO MUZZLE
YOUR MOUTH
Psalm 39

For Christians, part of growing *up* is growing *in* wisdom—a wisdom that helps us know when to speak and when to keep quiet. It allows us to determine whom we can trust and whom we can't. This type of wisdom, in a word, is called *discretion*. As Solomon wrote:

> My son, give attention to my wisdom,
> Incline your ear to my understanding;
> That you may observe *discretion*
> And your lips may reserve knowledge.
> (Prov. 5:1–2, emphasis added)

Let's face it, our mouths can get us into a lot of trouble. For instance, how many of us haven't accidentally blabbed someone else's secret? Or blurted out thoughts better left private? Or blasted someone in the heat of anger?

Discretion is especially difficult—and especially needed—when our emotions are running high. And seldom do our feelings run more strongly than when we are suffering.

When we're hurting badly, we sometimes long to cry out, to vent our rage and grief and confusion, to rail at heaven and tell God, "Back off and leave me alone! What am I to You?"

What should we do when we want to say these things—when our hearts, our bodies, or our lives are broken? Should we stuff these feelings down and pretend them away because "Christians shouldn't feel that way" or "it would be a bad witness"? Or should we bare our souls to anyone and everyone because Christians should live in truth?

Fortunately, we have more options than just these two. In Psalm 39, David embodies the dilemma of the struggling saint. His honest yet discreet response to his pain provides us with a way to wisely handle our hurts as well as our tongues.

Introduction to David's Psalm

In the superscription to this psalm, we learn that David entrusted the struggles of his heart to his friend Jeduthun, the director of Israel's choir. Two other prayer-songs, Psalms 62 and 77, were committed to Jeduthun as well. First Chronicles tells us that David appointed him and his six sons to make music to the Lord (16:41; 25:1–7). David obviously felt confident that Jeduthun could skillfully transpose the feeling of his words into music.

And David's feelings ran deep. He begged the Lord to hear his cry and not be silent at his tears (Ps. 39:12). Though we don't know the specific nature of David's distress,[1] it's clear that sorrow had a firm grip on his spirit. The anguish he communicated makes his psalm a *lament*—a poem that expresses "the sense of pain and letdown felt in suffering."[2]

A Song of Suffering

How did David deal with his sorrow? His first response was to try keeping it all inside.

Internal Struggle: "I Will Handle This on My Own"

David's opening words betrayed his mounting anguish:

> I said, "I will guard my ways
> That I may not sin with my tongue;
> I will guard my mouth as with a muzzle
> While the wicked are in my presence."
> I was mute and silent,
> I refrained even from good. (Psalm 39:1–2a)

As Derek Kidner observes, "David's feelings were running high enough to be taken for disloyalty if he had vented them in the wrong company."[3] He didn't want to give any ammunition to "the

---

1. Many commentators believe that an illness, or perhaps old age, prompted David to write this psalm. See Allen P. Ross, "Psalms," in *The Bible Knowledge Commentary*, Old Testament edition, ed. John F. Walvoord and Roy B. Zuck (Colorado Springs, Colo.: Chariot Victor Publishing, 1985), p. 823; J. A. Motyer, "The Psalms," in *New Bible Commentary: 21st Century Edition*, 4th ed., rev., ed. D. A. Carson, R. T. France, J. A. Motyer, and G. J. Wenham (Downers Grove, Ill.: InterVarsity Press, 1994), p. 511; John H. Stek, note on Psalm 39, in *The NIV Study Bible*, ed. Kenneth L. Barker (Grand Rapids, Mich.: Zondervan Bible Publishers, 1985), p. 825; and Peter C. Craigie, *Word Biblical Commentary: Psalms 1–50* (Waco, Tex.: Word Books, 1983), vol. 19, p. 307.

2. John Goldingay, "The Message of the Psalms," in *The Bible for Everyday Life*, ed. George Carey (Grand Rapids, Mich.: William B. Eerdmans Publishing Co., 1996), p. 92.

3. Derek Kidner, *Psalms 1–72: An Introduction and Commentary on Books I and II of the Psalms*, The Tyndale Old Testament Commentaries Series (Downers Grove, Ill.: InterVarsity Press, 1973), p. 156.

wicked"—those already hostile to the Lord and His ways. What was the outcome of this "pent-up protest"?[4]

> And my sorrow grew worse.
> My heart was hot within me,
> While I was musing the fire burned. (Ps. 39:2b–3a)

Like the ominous rumbling of a volcano, David's anguish demanded release. The pain of his heart needed to be expressed in words, so he unleashed his protest in prayer.

Prayer: "I Cannot Handle This Alone"

David's prayer first turned to how futile and fleeting he felt his life was:

> "Lord, make me to know my end
> And what is the extent of my days;
> Let me know how transient I am.
> Behold, You have made my days as handbreadths,
> And my lifetime as nothing in Your sight;
> Surely every man at his best is a mere breath. Selah.
> Surely every man walks about as a phantom;
> Surely they make an uproar for nothing;
> He amasses riches and does not know who will
>   gather them." (vv. 4–6)

Notice David's descriptions of his life: "transient," "nothing," "a mere breath," "a phantom." It's as though David were asking, *Lord, what meaning is there in such a short, struggle-filled life?* The Lord made his "days as handbreadths." A handbreadth was only four fingers wide—it was "one of the smallest measures in the Hebrew system of measuring."[5] The Hebrew word *hebel* is translated as "breath" in verse 5, as "for nothing" in verse 6, and as "mere breath" in verse 11. It emphasizes the depth of David's sense of hopelessness, serving "to expose the fatal insufficiency of all that is earthbound."[6]

---

4. Kidner, *Psalms 1–72,* p. 156.

5. Craigie, *Psalms 1–50,* p. 309.

6. Kidner, *Psalms 1–72,* p. 156.

Leslie Brandt's paraphrase captures the essence of David's impassioned entreaty:

O God, demonstrate some concern for me.
Give me some reason for this endless conflict,
    some objective for this fast-ebbing life of mine.
You made me what I am,
    and the span of my existence
    is but a speck of dust to You.
This is true about every human being.
A person is no more than a smidgen of moist air
    or a shadow without lasting substance.
Men and women endure this temporal turmoil
    for no reason whatsoever.
They agonize and toil
    only to leave the fruits for someone else to enjoy.[7]

Hope: "I Don't Want to Handle This Alone"

After wondering how a life that felt so miserably insignificant could have any meaning, David finally remembered that meaning is found in the Lord:

"And now, Lord, for what do I wait?
My hope is in You." (v. 7)

For the first time in David's psalm, a slender ray of sunlight pierced the dark, threatening skies. Hope warmed the chill of despair from David's spirit. David knew God could do for him what he couldn't do for himself.

Desperate Request: "Lord, You Handle This for Me"

Only God could forgive, cleanse, and have mercy on David's soul. Only God could set his situation right. So David begged the Lord:

"Deliver me from all my transgressions;
Make me not the reproach of the foolish.
I have become mute, I do not open my mouth,
Because it is You who have done it.

---

7. Leslie F. Brandt, *Psalms Now* (1974; reprint, St. Louis, Mo.: Concordia Publishing House, 1996), p. 68.

Remove Your plague from me;
Because of the opposition of Your hand I am perishing.
With reproofs You chasten a man for iniquity;
You consume as a moth what is precious to him;
Surely every man is a mere breath." Selah.
(vv. 8–11)

As we can see, David's struggle had no easy resolution. One prayer didn't "make it all better." He continued to struggle with what God was doing in his life, but *it was to God that he turned* to vent the frustration of his heart. And because he'd given this psalm to Jeduthun, the choir director, *it was also to God's people* that David revealed this honest reflection of his heart.

Broken and weary, David sought the balm of God's healing mercy in the last lines of his psalm:

"Hear my prayer, O Lord, and give ear to my cry;
Do not be silent at my tears;
For I am a stranger with You,
A sojourner like all my fathers.
Turn Your gaze away from me, that I may smile again
Before I depart and am no more." (vv. 12–13)

Whatever the cause of David's suffering—whether sin, the Lord's discipline, illness, or depression—his pain was real. At the end of his prayer, David was still in tears, still assuming that the Lord was angry with him and asking God to turn His disapproving face away so he could have some peace.

Yet David was still seeking the Lord. He wanted to see himself through God's eyes, to take on a new perspective. Recognizing that his time on earth was fleeting, he wanted to be known once again as "a man after God's own heart" (1 Sam. 13:14). He wanted the Lord's help. And he wanted to share his experience with God's people to help them through their suffering too.

Four Principles for Life

"The very presence of such prayers [as Psalm 39] in Scripture," Derek Kidner observes, "is a witness to His understanding. He knows how men speak when they are desperate."[8] God knows that

---

8. Kidner, *Psalms 1–72*, p. 157.

great pain is rarely accompanied by great discretion. And that's okay when we're pouring our hearts out to God. After all, He knows our hearts. We can be honest with Him. He will see us through and will give us the wisdom and discretion we need when relating our feelings to others.

David's psalm can teach us several things in relation to our speech.

First, *bottling things up inside is not the healthiest approach.* Sometimes we try to be stoic, fearing that expressing our sadness or confusion would be tantamount to not trusting God. But keeping everything inside, isolated and untreated, only makes our pain worse. We must be willing to pour out our hearts before God like David did.

Second, *blurting everything out indiscriminately can do more harm than good.* David was careful to keep quiet about his struggles when he was in the company of people who had turned away from God and His ways (v. 1). That's a good lesson for us to learn. Even in our suffering, we need to value the Lord's glory. Some people may use our doubts and frustrations as weapons, attacking our faith and challenging the Lord's credibility. Others who are trying to grapple with Who God is and what life is all about may stumble over our ill-placed confessions and limp away from God rather than toward Him.

Third, *bringing our honest thoughts and feelings to the Lord is always the right thing to do.* David brought all his despair and desperation to the Lord in this psalm, even begging God to let up on him (Ps. 39:10, 13). The Lord can handle our feelings—He knows our innermost souls much better than we do:

> O Lord, You have searched me and known me. . . .
> You understand my thought from afar. . . .
> Even before there is a word on my tongue,
> Behold, O Lord, You know it all. (Ps. 139:1a, 2b, 4)

Fourth, *being open about our struggles benefits ourselves and others.* David didn't leave this psalm of prayer in his private journal. Instead, he brought it to Jeduthun, who would bring it to the faithful worshipers of Yahweh in Israel. Perhaps some in that congregation needed David's words to express what was in their own hearts. Perhaps Jeduthun and the people prayed for their hurting king. Just remember, the context in which David bared his heart was the community of faith, in the company of other believers. The Lord meant for His church to be a safe place for the hurting, a strengthening place for the weak. How well are we living up to His plan?

When it comes to sharing our struggles, sometimes we may need to muzzle our mouths, but more often than not, we probably just need a little direction. And God's Word, honest and direct as it is, is the best place to get it.

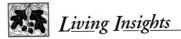 *Living Insights*

Tuesday, September 11, 2001, began as a normal workday for most Americans. But the events that unfolded that morning forever changed the skyline of New York City and the hearts and lives of people around the world. Millions watched in horror as hijacked planes destroyed the twin towers of the World Trade Center and crashed into the Pentagon. Images of burning buildings—buildings that represented the dreams, hopes, and ideals of the American people—were forever seared in our collective memory.

One monumental event is all it takes to make us realize how fleeting life is. As James notes:

> Come now, you who say, "Today or tomorrow we will go to such and such a city, and spend a year there and engage in business and make a profit." Yet you do not know what your life will be like tomorrow. You are just a vapor that appears for a little while and then vanishes away. (James 4:13–14)

Life brings with it no guarantees. But, like David, we can trust that God is in control and that He works all things for good to those who love Him and who are called according to His purpose (Rom. 8:28).

The way you spend your time is a direct reflection of your priorities. Think about an "average day" in your life. Ask yourself the following questions: How much of my day is devoted to spending time with God? What steps can I take to make my time with my heavenly Father more of a priority?

_____

_____

_____

_____

Who encourages me to spend time with God and to pursue my relationship with Him more passionately? How do those people motivate me?

_____

_____

_____

_____

Who are the people I turn to when I face difficult issues? What are the qualities they have that I admire? When they know that I am facing a trial, how do they respond?

_____

_____

_____

_____

When friends confess a struggle or discuss a painful situation with me, how can I encourage them? What comfort can I offer them from God's Word? How can I change my responses to others to reflect an eternal perspective?

_____

_____

_____

_____

Digging Deeper

It's quite possible that David was undergoing the *discipline* of the Lord when he wrote this psalm. Let's take a moment to understand God's discipline from a biblical perspective.

The Bible gives us examples of four main areas of discipline. First, God disciplines individual believers who have fallen into sin. Second, He reprimands the wayward nation of Israel. Third, believers are taught how to implement disciplinary measures in the local church. Fourth, the Bible illustrates how parents are to correct and guide their children.[9]

What is the purpose of these disciplinary measures? They are meant to give believers an opportunity to repent and turn from their sin in order that they might be restored to fellowship with God.

Of course, discipline often involves pain and chastisement. But it is important to understand that the pain and suffering caused by God's discipline are not meant to be an end in themselves. Rather, His discipline is a means to bring about change in our lives, shape our character, and bring us back to Him (see Heb. 12:3–12).[10]

Pruning, on the other hand, is distinct from discipline. Bruce Wilkinson notes in his book *Secrets of the Vine*, "God's strategy for coaxing a greater harvest out of His branches is . . . for you to cut away immature commitments and lesser priorities to make room for even greater abundance."[11]

The difference between *discipline* and *pruning* lies in their causes. Discipline results from our sin. But pruning comes when we're doing something *right*! When believers bear fruit, God prunes the vines of our lives to allow us to be even more fruitful and productive. He cuts away the parts of ourselves that hinder us from living an abundant life in Him. Pruning is a growth process—and growth is often accompanied by growing pains!

God wants us to live the most abundant lives possible, so He prunes us to allow us to yield even more fruit for Him. He cuts away the dead wood in our lives so our vines can blossom forth with blessing, holiness, joy, righteousness, and peace.

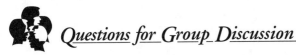 *Questions for Group Discussion*

1. As you read through Psalm 39, to which of David's emotions could you best relate? Have you ever become frustrated with God? What were the circumstances? What helped you get through that struggle?

9. Wendell Johnston, "Discipline," in *The Theological Wordbook*, ed. Charles R. Swindoll (Nashville, Tenn.: Word Publishing, 2000), pp. 95–97.

10. Wendell Johnston, "Discipline," in *The Theological Wordbook*.

11. Bruce Wilkinson, *Secrets of the Vine* (Sisters, Ore.: Multnomah Publishers, 2001), pp. 57–58.

2. What role did prayer play in David's life, especially in this time of intense anguish? What are some theological truths you learn about human life and about God from David's psalm?

3. Is all adversity a sign of sin in someone's life? Read John 9:1–3 and 1 Corinthians 11:27–32. What do these New Testament passages teach about the Lord's discipline in our lives? How should we respond to others who are experiencing adversity?

4. A major theme in Psalm 39 is the brevity of life. Read through Psalm 90 and Ecclesiastes 2:2–3. How do these passages relate to David's struggle against futility? How does your relationship with Christ bring you meaning in life?

Chapter 8

WHEN IS IT
RIGHT TO FIGHT?

Selected Scriptures

To fight or not to fight?

Christians have grappled with that frequently-asked and rarely-settled question for generations. The response has wide implications —from the youngster struggling to defend himself against the school-yard bully, to Christian citizens taking up arms to defend their country, to believers taking a stand against laws that dishonor God.

Is it right to fight? If so, when? And when are believers to "turn the other cheek" and walk away?

To answer these questions, we must resist merely falling back on popular opinion, parental advice, worldly wisdom, or cultural influence. Instead, we must seek the guidance of God's Word to gain a solid foothold on these slippery issues.

Old Testament Perspective

Did you know that the Bible uses the words *fight, fighting, war, warfare, kill,* and other related words more than 400 times? Since the Lord has given considerable attention to these issues, we need to listen closely to what He has said.

Perhaps the most central guideline He has provided for us is the sixth commandment:

"You shall not murder." (Exod. 20:13)

"Murder"? That's right. Most of us are probably more familiar with the King James rendering—"Thou shalt not kill"—but the Hebrew verb is actually more specific. *Rāsah* generally refers to any form of unlawful taking of human life. This ranges from manslaughter to vicious acts of revenge to premeditated murder. Whatever the case, the commandment makes clear that God's will is for the preservation and sanctity of human life.[1]

---

1. See R. Laird Harris, Gleason L. Archer, Jr., and Bruce K. Waltke, eds., *Theological Wordbook of the Old Testament* (Chicago, Ill.: Moody Press, 1980), vol. 2, p. 860. Commentator John I.

Life is so sacred, in fact, that the Lord not only sanctioned but prescribed the death penalty for the crime of murder:

"Whoever sheds man's blood,
By man his blood shall be shed,
For in the image of God
He made man." (Gen. 9:6)

"He who strikes a man so that he dies shall surely be put to death." (Exod. 21:12)

From this we learn that certain instances of killing, such as capital punishment done in justice, are not violations of God's command prohibiting murder.

What about war? Does *rāsah* apply to the battlefield? Does God unilaterally oppose all human warfare? Based on the study of various biblical uses of *rāsah*, it seems that this term does not apply to warfare. But the answer to these questions is complex, and we can't do it justice in this single study.[2] We can see, however, that the Lord fought with and for His people in Old Testament times:

They [certain Israelites] cried out to God in the battle, and He answered their prayers because they trusted in Him. . . . For many fell slain, because *the war was of God.* (1 Chron. 5:20b, 22a, emphasis added; see also Num. 25:16–18a; 31:3)

Blessed be the Lord, my rock,
Who trains my hands for war,
And my fingers for battle. (Ps. 144:1)

God not only supported the warring acts of men who fought for righteousness and the Lord's cause, but He actually directed the battle and determined the victor.

This certainly does not mean that God relishes the terrible suffering associated with war. Isaiah characterized God's future

---

Durham adds that *rāsah* "is an act of killing, premeditated or not, related to vengeance or not, that violates the standard of living Yahweh expects of those who have given themselves to him." *Word Biblical Commentary: Exodus* (Waco, Tex.: Word Books, Publisher, 1987), vol. 3, p. 293.

2. For further study, we recommend *War: Four Christian Views,* ed. Robert G. Clouse (Downers Grove, Ill.: InterVarsity Press, 1981).

reign as follows:

> And He will judge between the nations,
> And will render decisions for many peoples;
> And they will hammer their swords into plowshares
>   and their spears into pruning hooks.
> Nation will not lift up sword against nation,
> And never again will they learn war. (Isa. 2:4)

For the time being, however, we still live in a sinful world, and warfare is part of God's sovereign plan for godly individuals to stand against the enemies of righteousness.

If standing against those enemies requires civil disobedience, that, too, may be sanctioned by God. This is seen in two Old Testament illustrations: the stories of Daniel and his three friends Shadrach, Meshach, and Abed-nego. Captured and taken to Babylon as teens, these godly and intelligent young Jewish men were chosen to serve in the court of King Nebuchadnezzar. The trouble started when the king built an enormous golden image, possibly of himself, and commanded that everyone in the kingdom bow down and worship it (Dan. 3:1–5). If anyone refused, he or she would be thrown into "a furnace of blazing fire" (v. 6).

Shadrach, Meshach, and Abed-nego, however, worshiped the One true God and could neither disobey Him nor bow down to a lie (v. 12; see also Exod. 20:3–5; Isa. 44:9–20; 45:20). The enraged king arrogantly asked them, "What god is there who can deliver you out of my hands?" (Dan. 3:15b). And he had the furnace made seven times hotter and threw them into the fire. But the Lord honored their faith, answering Nebuchadnezzar's egotistical question by standing with His people and preserving them. Their clothing didn't even have the faintest smell of smoke (vv. 19–27)!

The result? Nebuchadnezzar himself blessed the Lord and decreed that everyone else give Him honor too (vv. 28–30).

Daniel faced his test years later, when power had passed from Babylon to the Medes and Persians. Though times and kings had changed, hatred for the Jews had not. A group of jealous officials persuaded King Darius to pass a law forbidding anyone to make "a petition to any god or man besides [the] king, for thirty days"—with any person who broke this law being "cast into the lions' den" (6:7).

But Daniel knew that only one God existed, and he continued to pray to Him three times a day with his windows open toward Jerusalem, just as he had always done (v. 10). For this act of civil disobedience, the faithful and honest Daniel was thrown into the den of lions (v. 16).

The Lord, however, honored Daniel's stand and protected His servant, as Daniel himself told his friend the king:

> "O king, live forever! My God sent His angel and shut the lions' mouths and they have not harmed me, inasmuch as I was found innocent before Him; and also toward you, O king, I have committed no crime." (vv. 21–22)

Respectful to the king he loyally served, Daniel nevertheless spoke the truth plainly, declaring his innocence to Darius. The grateful king listened and punished Daniel's accusers with the punishment they had sought for Daniel (v. 24). And the king made a declaration of his own:

> "I make a decree that in all the dominion of my kingdom men are to fear and tremble before the God of Daniel;
> For He is the living God and enduring forever,
> And His kingdom is one which will not be destroyed,
> And His dominion will be forever.
> He delivers and rescues and performs signs and wonders
> In heaven and on earth,
> Who has also delivered Daniel from the power of the lions." (vv. 26–27)

Because of Daniel's faithful stand against a government that had overstepped its God-given bounds (compare Rom. 13:1–7), the Lord was honored throughout an entire nation!

From all of these Old Testament examples, we can see that God authorized killing in certain circumstances, set aside certain times for war, and blessed people's recognition of His ultimate authority.

But do these Old Testament principles hold true under the New Covenant of Jesus Christ?

New Testament Perspective

The New Testament also supports a bold faith that stands against what's false and evil, as both Jesus and the apostles displayed.

Jesus versus the Pharisees

Matthew 22 records a pointed confrontation between Jesus and the Pharisees. Wanting to trap Jesus between disloyalty to the Jews and treason toward Rome, the Pharisees asked Him, "Tell us then, what do You think? Is it lawful to give a poll-tax to Caesar, or not?" (v. 17). Jesus got right to the point:

> But Jesus perceived their malice, and said, "Why are you testing Me, you hypocrites? Show Me the coin used for the poll-tax." And they brought Him a denarius. And He said to them, "Whose likeness and inscription is this?" They said to Him, "Caesar's." Then He said to them, "Then render to Caesar the things that are Caesar's; and to God the things that are God's."[3] And hearing this, they were amazed, and leaving Him, they went away. (vv. 18–22)

Let's notice several things in Jesus' handling of this situation. First, He faced the truth: He "perceived their malice." He didn't try to pretend that things were nicer than they were, nor did He ignore the dark spiritual undercurrents flowing from His enemies.

Second, He cut to the core of their sin with a strong rebuke: "you hypocrites." Jesus was humble and gentle at heart, but He was no spiritual doormat to be trampled underfoot.

And third, in His counsel to give Caesar what belonged to him, Jesus upheld the responsibility believers have to the law of the land as well as to the law of God. In contrast to some Christians' opinions today, Jesus was not anti-government, but anti-evil.

Jesus did not look the other way when faced with evil. He confronted it directly. Think of how He angrily sent the money-changers in the temple scrambling (John 2:13–17). Or consider His diatribe in Matthew 23 against the religious leaders (or *misleaders*) of His day. He punctuated His rebukes with such phrases as:

- "Woe to you, scribes and Pharisees, hypocrites . . ." (vv. 13,

---

3. Commentator R. T. France notes, "In getting them to show him a *denarius*, . . . Jesus exposed them as *hypocrites*, since no patriotic Jew should have been carrying this coin, with its 'idolatrous' *portrait* of the emperor and its inscription giving him the title 'Son of God.' If they were using *Caesar's* money, let them pay his poll-tax! Jesus thus . . . implied that loyalty to a pagan government was not incompatible with loyalty to God." "Matthew," in *New Bible Commentary: 21st Century Edition*, 4th ed., rev., ed. D. A. Carson, R. T. France, J. A. Motyer, and G. J. Wenham (Downers Grove, Ill.: InterVarsity Press, 1994), p. 933.

14, 15, 23, 25, 27, 29)

- "Woe to you, blind guides . . ." (vv. 16, 24)

- "You fools and blind men!" (v. 17)

- "You are like whitewashed tombs . . . full of dead men's bones and all uncleanness." (v. 27)

- "You serpents, you brood of vipers, how will you escape the sentence of hell?" (v. 33)

Clearly, Jesus' obedience to His Father in heaven forced Him to challenge this evil abuse of power. Human souls were at stake, and so was the honor of His Father.

The Apostles

Fueled by the power of the Holy Spirit, the apostles blazed through the biblical world proclaiming the gospel of Christ. Opposition was inevitable, so early on they had to take a stand. In Acts 3, we find Peter and John having healed a lame beggar (vv. 1–10). After preaching to the crowds and glorifying Christ, Peter and John were arrested by the Sadducees and temple guard (3:11–4:12). After a night in jail and an interrogation, the apostles were ordered by the Sanhedrin "not to speak or teach at all in the name of Jesus" (4:18).

Their response?

> But Peter and John answered and said to them, "Whether it is right in the sight of God to give heed to you rather than to God, you be the judge; for we cannot stop speaking about what we have seen and heard." (vv. 19–20)

Despite further threats and another arrest (v. 21; 5:17–28), the apostles did not waver in their allegiance. They chose to serve their Higher Authority, the Lord God: "We must obey God rather than men" (5:29).

Suggestions for Today

How do we apply these historical lessons to our contemporary world? Let's consider them in the context of three different arenas.

In the Personal Realm

As believers, we are to have an attitude of humility, gentleness, and submission toward our neighbors. But do we honor God by surrendering to injustice at every turn? Definitely not! Let's see what the Bible has to say about self-defense.

The Old Testament Law allowed a man to defend his home and family during a robbery, considering him not guilty if he killed the intruder (Exod. 22:2). Self-defense was also permitted in Nehemiah 4:13–23, when Nehemiah directed those building the wall to work with one hand and hold a weapon in the other to defend themselves against enemies. In Esther 8 and 9, the Jews were permitted to defend themselves against the attack brought against them by Haman's decree. And throughout the Psalms, David refers to incidents where he rightly defended himself and the nation of Israel against the enemies of God.

From these biblical accounts, we can conclude that God doesn't condemn His people when they act out of self-defense.

In the Civil Realm

As Christians, we are to humbly submit to the laws and leadership of our government. However, obedience to the Lord is our ultimate obligation, and there may be times when we are compelled to defy earthly authority for spiritual reasons.

If we are called to take such a stand, we are to do so with the spirit and humility of Christ. Here's how the apostle Peter put it:

> Submit yourselves for the Lord's sake to every human institution, whether to a king as the one in authority, or to governors as sent by him for the punishment of evildoers and the praise of those who do right. For such is the will of God that by doing right you may silence the ignorance of foolish men. Act as free men, and do not use your freedom as a covering for evil, but use it as bondslaves of God. Honor all people, love the brotherhood, fear God, honor the king. (1 Pet. 2:13–17)

What does this mean in the case of our nation going to war against another? If believers are called on to defend their country's interests and are confident that to do so would not compromise their obedience to God, then serving in the military is in accordance with God's Word.

In the Spiritual Realm

As Christians, obedience to the Lord is our ultimate obligation. Jesus and the apostles are our models in this area. As Peter wrote:

> Sanctify Christ as Lord in your hearts, always being ready to make a defense to everyone who asks you to give an account for the hope that is in you, yet with gentleness and reverence. (1 Pet. 3:15; see also 2 Tim. 2:25; James 1:19–20)

Concluding Exhortations

Let's keep in mind several important truths as we close this study.

First, *there is a difference between standing for what is right and having a belligerent attitude.* Gentleness, meekness, humility, and love are marks of a genuine follower of Christ. These character qualities are not to be laid aside whenever we're compelled to defend the cause of righteousness (Phil. 2:3–8).

Second, *there is no guarantee of safety or divine deliverance when we fight for the truth.* For every Daniel who emerges unscathed by the jaws of persecution, countless millions suffer undeservedly for standing for truth. Hebrews 11:35–40 describes the brutal treatment of Christians who have suffered for their beliefs down through the ages. But regardless of the consequences, we must remember that we are on the right side and that God has promised to never forsake us (Heb. 13:5).

Finally, *exercise spiritual discernment when the need to defend the truth presents itself.* Fighting should never be our first course of action. We should attempt to resolve conflicts peacefully, if at all possible. However, as Jesus demonstrated, sometimes confrontation is necessary in order to stand up for God's truth and defend the faith.

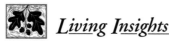 *Living Insights*

We often envision the battle between good and evil as a kind of cosmic *Star Wars*, with God as "the Force" defending goodness and truth, and Satan as the evil "Empire," representing the forces of the "Dark Side." But it's important to *deepen* our understanding of spiritual warfare so that we will be prepared to stand firm against the enemy's clever assaults. In the book of Ephesians, Paul exhorts:

> Put on the full armor of God, so that you will be able
> to stand firm against the schemes of the devil. For
> our struggle is not against flesh and blood, but against
> the rulers, against the powers, against the world
> forces of this darkness, against the spiritual forces of
> wickedness in the heavenly places. (6:11–12)

According to these verses, we are not fighting a battle against earthly powers, but against spiritual powers. How have you experienced spiritual warfare? How have you sensed Satan's aggression?

_____

_____

_____

_____

_____

According to Ephesians 6:14–17a, how can we prepare for battle? What are our defenses against the Enemy?

_____

_____

_____

_____

Verse 17b describes our only weapon for spiritual warfare. What is it? What are some ways you can use this weapon to defeat Satan in your life?

_____

_____

_____

_____

 *Questions for Group Discussion*

1. Spend some time discussing your views on the issue of when it's right for Christians to fight. In what ways have your views changed after interacting with biblical teaching?

2. How would you witness to a non-Christian who has expressed concern about the biblical stories of God's involvement in warfare? How would the issues of righteousness and God's holiness contribute to your discussion?

3. Do you believe there is biblical support for the death penalty as part of the modern judicial system? How would you defend your view using Scripture?

4. To what extent should Christians employ political and diplomatic means to resolve challenges to religious freedom? Is there ever any justification for taking up arms to defend Christian values? Explain your answer.

5. How seriously do you feel Christians take the threat of spiritual enemies as described in Ephesians 6? What steps can believers take to prepare for and protect themselves from spiritual attacks?

6. What does Paul mean when he exhorts Timothy in 1 Timothy 6:12 to "fight the good fight"? Jude also uses this language in exhorting believers to "contend" or "fight" for the faith. What does this mean? Do you ever feel like you are "contending for the faith"? If so, in what ways?

Chapter 9

NO SUBSTITUTE
FOR WORSHIP
Isaiah 6:1–8

Whatever happened to worship? A.W. Tozer observed that worship
is the missing jewel in modern evangelicalism. We're
organized; we work; we have our agendas. We have
almost everything, but there's one thing that the
churches, even the gospel churches, do not have:
that is the ability to worship. We are not cultivating
the art of worship. It's the one shining gem that is
lost to the modern church, and I believe that we
ought to search for this until we find it.[1]

Worship—our glorious missing jewel. Without it, our church
experience is like a beautiful engagement ring that has lost its
diamond. Structure without beauty. Mere activity instead of awe.
Such is the state of modern Christianity. Without worship, we're just
"playing church" instead of truly entering into the presence of God.

We say, "Amen, brother!" when the sermon's good. Jump up
and clap our hands—look the part of impassioned praise. Stand up,
sit down, kneel, and pray. Eyes closed, head bowed, look somber
and contrite. Here comes the offering plate—dutifully drop in a
dollar. Last song. Shake the pastor's hand. "Want to go out for
lunch?" "Where did I put my keys?"

Where did we put God?

It's amazing that we can be in God's house all morning and
sometimes never see Him, never worship, in the midst of our routine.

Do you long for a deeper relationship with the living God? Do
you sense that there is something more powerful and precious to

---

This chapter has been adapted from "Discovering the Missing Jewel of Worship," in the Bible
study guide *Making New Discoveries*, written by Gary Matlack, from the Bible-teaching
ministry of Charles R. Swindoll (Anaheim, Calif.: Insight for Living, 1995), pp. 29–36.

1. A. W. Tozer, "Worship: The Normal Employment of Moral Beings," in *The Best of A. W.
Tozer*, comp. Warren W. Wiersbe (Grand Rapids, Mich.: Baker Book House, 1978; reprint,
Camp Hill, Pa.: Christian Publications, 1991), pp. 217–18.

be found? Then grab your flashlight and let's find this dazzling gem, study it, and see how we can restore it to its rightful place.

Worship Illuminated

The authors of *Worship: Rediscovering the Missing Jewel* shine a light on what worship really is:

> *Worship is an active response to God whereby we declare His worth.* Worship is not passive, but is participative. Worship is not simply a mood; it is a response. Worship is not just a feeling; it is a declaration. . . .
>
> The English word worship is wonderfully expressive of the act that it describes. This term comes from the Anglo-Saxon *weorthscipe*, which then was modified to *worthship*, and finally to *worship*. Worship means "to attribute worth" to something or someone.[2]

Ascribing to God His supreme worth—that's the dazzling gem that has been snatched from its setting. We often focus on the preacher's worth, the teachers' worth, the music's worth, the building's worth—even the nursery's worth! And all of these are important. But too often, we stop there and fail to allow these elements to usher us into the presence of God. Our tendency is to look at *them* instead of *Him*.

How can we restore this priceless gem, this declaration of God's immeasurable worth, to our churches today? Let's learn from the prophet Isaiah, whose experience of worship forever changed his life.

Isaiah's Worship Experience

Any jewel sparkles more brightly against a dark backdrop, and the jewel of worship is no exception. In Isaiah's day, the backdrop was Judah, a nation that had turned its back on God. Empowered by military might and financial security, the Jewish people felt that they no longer needed Yahweh. Presumption had replaced gratitude. Pride had usurped reverence.

Judah's King Uzziah personified this attitude when he brazenly entered the temple to burn incense—a duty reserved solely for

---

2. Ronald Allen and Gordon Borror, *Worship: Rediscovering the Missing Jewel* (Portland, Oreg.: Multnomah Press, 1982), p. 16.

priests. As a result, God struck the proud king with leprosy, and Uzziah lived out the rest of his life in shameful quarantine (see 2 Chron. 26:16–23). Uzziah's godly son Jotham took the throne after his death, but the nation of Judah "continued acting corruptly" (27:2).

It's against this dark backdrop that Isaiah entered—as the prophet who would restore the luster of worship to Judah.

He Saw the Lord

> In the year of King Uzziah's death I saw the Lord sitting on a throne, lofty and exalted, with the train of His robe filling the temple. Seraphim stood above Him, each having six wings: with two he covered his face, and with two he covered his feet, and with two he flew. (Isa. 6:1–2)

The Jewish people had lost sight of God. So it was significant that Isaiah's worship experience began with a stunning vision of the living Lord on His throne, surrounded by angels! God was "lofty and exalted"—His glory filled the entire temple. His presence was so holy that even the seraphim covered their faces, indicating their humility before God as they lifted up praises around His throne.

These six-winged angelic beings appear only in Isaiah 6:2–6. The term *seraph* comes from the Hebrew word *sarap*, which means "to burn." One scholar notes, "These angelic beings were brilliant as flaming fire, symbolic of the purity and power of the heavenly court."[3] Not only were these glorious beings, they were ardent in their worship of the Lord:

> And one called out to another and said,
> "Holy, Holy, Holy, is the Lord of hosts,
> The whole earth is full of His glory."
> And the foundations of the thresholds trembled at
> the voice of him who called out, while the temple
> was filling with smoke. (vv. 3–4)

This celestial worship service literally rocked the foundations of the temple! The angels thundered, "Holy, Holy, Holy" in their litany of praise. Their repetition of the word *holy* three times signifies infinite magnitude or duration. "The Lord of hosts," they cry out, "is infinitely majestic and holy."

---

3. R. Laird Harris, Gleason L. Archer, and Bruce K. Waltke, eds., *Theological Worldbook of the Old Testament* (Chicago, Ill.: Moody Press, 1980), vol. 2, p. 884.

Worship, then, begins with our eyes fixed on the holy Lord of heaven. When we come to church for worship, we should be looking for God. Our hearts should be attuned to His heart, our souls open to drink in His glory.

Unfortunately, we're often surrounded by distractions that drag us down from the heavenlies—even in church. Memories of a breakfast spat with our spouse or plans for this week's big presentation at the office swirl around in our minds. Not to mention the people who fill the pews—Mr. Johnson with his bad breath, the Mitchell twins making confetti out of the church bulletin, and that lady behind us with the sniffles.

Satan does everything he can to keep us from focusing on the majesty of God. So we must come with our spiritual eyes open, looking for the Lord in the message, the music, and the fellowship.

He Was Touched by the Lord

> Then I said,
> "Woe is me, for I am ruined!
> Because I am a man of unclean lips,
> And I live among a people of unclean lips;
> For my eyes have seen the King, the Lord of
> hosts." (v. 5)

The brilliant light of God's countenance revealed the darkness and desperation of Isaiah's condition. "I am ruined!" he cried out. "I am a man of unclean lips, living among a people of unclean lips!" In other words, he was a sinner living among sinners.[4] How else could he respond when confronted face-to-face with God's holiness?

The Lord, however, didn't abandon Isaiah because of his sinfulness. He cleansed him in a unique way:

> Then one of the seraphim flew to me with a burning
> coal in his hand, which he had taken from the altar
> with tongs. He touched my mouth with it and said,
> "Behold, this has touched your lips; and your iniquity
> is taken away and your sin is forgiven." (vv. 6–7)

---

4. Isaiah, though greatly used by God, still had a sinful nature, as did the people to whom he ministered. Commentators generally agree that the prophet's admission of "unclean lips" signifies his awareness of his sinful nature in light of God's holiness. "Unclean lips," however, might also indicate that Isaiah struggled with a particular sin of the tongue, such as profanity, which he needed to confess to receive God's cleansing.

God touched Isaiah with the cleansing fire of forgiveness. This shows that worship isn't something to be checked off our religious "to do" list; it's an experience God uses to meet us at our point of need. After beholding God's glory, Isaiah saw his own sinfulness more clearly than ever. He, like all of us, needed hope that a sinful human could stand before a holy God without fear of judgment.

Notice that the seraph flew to Isaiah with the burning coal in his hand. Isaiah didn't reach out to God—God reached out to Him. The Holy reached out to the hopeless. The Light penetrated the darkness. And just as God forgave Isaiah, He also provided forgiveness for all of us through His Son, Jesus Christ. One commentator notes:

> In the presence of the Lord, we are all unclean and even the fiery seraphim are not clean before Him or worthy to behold Him. How fortunate, however, that Christ as the Priestly King has not only an exalted *throne*, but also an *altar*, where sins can be burned away, as happened with this seer.[5]

Because of Jesus Christ, we can approach God without being consumed by His holiness. Just as God sent the seraph to cleanse Isaiah's lips, He sent Christ to cleanse our hearts and to open the door to God's throne room so we can approach Him with our requests as well as our worship.

He Heard from the Lord

> Then I heard the voice of the Lord, saying, "Whom shall I send, and who will go for Us?" (v. 8a)

Isaiah heard the voice of the Lord offering him a chance to serve as God's messenger to the nation. He had just been made aware of the depths of his sinfulness, and now he was being shown that he was useful and valuable to God. How gracious of God to come close to Isaiah and affirm his value and usefulness!

Worship, for us, also reinforces our sense of purpose. We praise God, confess our sins, and evaluate our lives as He speaks to our hearts. So we must *listen*. We never know which part of the worship service God might use to enlighten us, convict us, or stir us to action.

---

5. Harry Bultema, *Commentary on Isaiah*, trans. Cornelius Lambregtse (Muskegon, Mich.: Bereer Publishing, 1923, Grand Rapids, Mich.: Kregel Publications, 1981), p. 96.

He Responded to the Lord

Then I said, "Here am I. Send me!" (v. 8b)

Eager and grateful to his awesome yet tender God, Isaiah shouted "Me! I'll go for you. Please send me!" So God honored his willing heart by making Isaiah the bearer of His Word and of great prophecies concerning the coming of the Messiah. It was through him that the people heard:

"A virgin will be with child." (7:14)

"The people who walk in darkness
Will see a great light." (9:2)

"Those who wait for the Lord . . . will mount up
with wings like eagles." (40:31)

"My thoughts are not your thoughts,
Neither are your ways My ways." (55:8)

Isaiah's experience demonstrates that worship doesn't end with simply *listening* to God. It also calls for a response on our part. And who knows? God just may use us to be an Isaiah for our age— bringing good news to the afflicted, binding up the brokenhearted, proclaiming freedom to captives, and comforting those who mourn (see 61:1–2).

Three Principles for Worship

Clearly, there's no substitute for worship in our lives. We must hold tightly to this glimmering jewel to keep from losing it again. These three principles will help us.

First, *a deep sense of need prompts worship.* God created us; He understands that we all have deep-seated needs. He designed worship for people who need Him. Worshiping God in His holiness and majesty helps us to see ourselves as we truly are—sinful and in need of a Savior. It gives God the opportunity to display His strength through our weakness.

Second, *preoccupation with the Lord enhances worship.* The Almighty God is the object of our worship. We must preoccupy ourselves with *Him.* Not the pastor. Not the music. Not the building. Not the programs. These are all simply means to an end, which is worshiping God in spirit and in truth. Spend some time in personal worship before you attend your next church service, perhaps on

Saturday night or early Sunday morning. Read the Bible, sing, pray, reflect. Then enter the sanctuary with one goal in mind—to meet God and continue your worship.

Third, *honesty, humility, and availability are vital to worship.* Worship is a time to open up, not cover up. It's a time for confession, not excuses. God knows our needs anyway, so why try to hide them? Sometimes we need to come to Him and humbly confess, "Lord, I don't have it all together. I need to see you. I need to hear from you." When we do, He will restore the beautiful jewel of worship to its proper place in our lives.

 Living Insights

The book of Luke tells the story of two sisters, Martha and Mary. One was a worker, and the other was a worshiper:

> . . . A woman named Martha welcomed [Jesus] into her home. She had a sister called Mary, who was seated at the Lord's feet, listening to His word. But Martha was distracted with all her preparations; and she came up to Him and said, "Lord, do You not care that my sister has left me to do all the serving alone? Then tell her to help me." But the Lord answered and said to her, "Martha, Martha, you are worried and bothered about so many things; but only one thing is necessary, for Mary has chosen the good part, which shall not be taken away from her." (10:38b–42)

Martha was the worker, always wanting to do things right. She opened her home to Jesus, but then busied herself with the details. She concerned herself with propriety, appearance, timeliness, and orderliness. But in the midst of all her preparations, she lost sight of what mattered most—spending time at the feet of Jesus.

Mary, on the other hand, was the worshiper—content to stop *doing* and just *be*. Mary was less concerned with doing things right than she was with doing the right things. As a result, she was able to tune out distractions and focus her attention on Christ.

In light of this story, ask yourself the following questions: Do I tend to be more like Martha or Mary? In what ways?

_____

_____

_____

_____

_____

What are the preparations and/or distractions that sometimes keep me from focusing my attention on Christ?

_____

_____

_____

_____

_____

Can I eliminate some of these to allow myself more time to concentrate on Him? If so, which ones?

_____

_____

_____

_____

_____

What practical steps can I take to renew a sense of worship in my daily life?

_____

_____

_____

_____

_____

 *Questions for Group Discussion*

1. Spend some time discussing common attitudes about worship. Did you have a concept of worship growing up? What was it? How was it modeled in the church? How was it modeled in your family? How was it modeled in the world?

2. What is worship like in your church now? What steps do you take to maintain your personal time with the Lord and your own sense of worship? What can you do to enhance your corporate worship?

3. Share one of your most meaningful worship experiences. Where were you? What happened? How did God speak to you?

4. What distracts you from being able to worship in personal settings? In group settings? How can you make changes to eliminate these distractions and experience more meaningful worship?

5. Read John 4:7–30. Who are the main characters? What is the issue at stake? What does worshiping "in spirit and in truth" mean to you, personally?

Chapter 10

FRESH FRUIT FROM
LIPS OF PRAISE
Psalm 116

When she was fifteen years old, Elizabeth Barrett suffered a debilitating spinal injury and became partially disabled. Forced to spend much of her time indoors, she read voraciously and grew to become a brilliant scholar and author. When poet Robert Browning wrote to express his admiration for her poems, she began exchanging letters with him. The couple fell deeply in love and married in 1846. Four years later, Elizabeth Barrett Browning wrote one of the most exquisite and well-known love poems in the English language. "Sonnet 43" begins:

> How do I love thee? Let me count the ways.
> I love thee to the depth and breadth and height
> My soul can reach . . .[1]

Psalm 116 is also an extraordinary expression of love—addressed to God! "How do I love Thee, God?" the psalmist seems to ask. In his answers, we find several magnificent truths about God's goodness and deliverance. Let's discover what motivated the psalmist to pen this sonnet of love to the Lord.

God's Goodness Toward Us

The psalm opens with the simplest and most universal words of affection: "I love the Lord" (v. 1a). This uniquely personal expression of emotion seems to burst forth from the psalmist's heart. He can hardly contain his feelings, and he unashamedly proclaims them to whoever might listen.

Such passion immediately draws our curiosity. What underground spring feeds the psalmist's overflowing fountain of praise? What has God done for him to move his soul?

---

1. Elizabeth Barrett Browning, "Sonnet 43," http://www.gale.com/freresrc/poets_cn/s43.htm, accessed on September 28, 2001.

He Hears Me

> I love the Lord, because He hears
> My voice and my supplications.
> Because He has inclined His ear to me,
> Therefore I shall call upon Him as long as I live.
> (vv. 1–2)

He offers the first reason in verses 1–2, in which he says, in effect, "*I love Him because He hears me when I call on Him.*" The Hebrew word *natah*, translated *inclined* in verse 2, means "to bend or turn aside."[2] In essence, the psalmist is saying, "God 'bends an ear' when I call on Him."

Do you ever wonder whether God truly hears your prayers? The weight of an ongoing trial may be sinking your once-buoyant confidence in God. Setbacks, roadblocks, and disappointments may cause you to doubt God's power. And broken dreams may cause you to question His love.

David, who wrote many of the Psalms, knew what it was like to go through the valleys of life. But he also experienced the restoration and forgiveness that only God could provide. His encouragement in Psalm 40 is to wait for the Lord, whose timing is always perfect:

> I waited patiently for the Lord;
> And He inclined to me and heard my cry.
> He brought me up out of the pit of destruction, out
>   of the miry clay,
> And He set my feet upon a rock making my footsteps
>   firm.
> He put a new song in my mouth, a song of praise
>   to our God;
> Many will see and fear
> And will trust in the Lord. (vv. 1–3)

When we trust that God hears our prayers, when we have confidence that He is listening, we can trust that He will also answer—in His own time.

---

2. Francis Brown, S. R. Driver, and Charles A. Briggs, eds., *The Brown-Driver-Briggs Hebrew and English Lexicon* (Peabody, Mass.: Hendrickson Publishers, 2000), p. 639–40.

He Rescues Me

The composer of Psalm 116 goes on to explore the specifics of God's answer to prayer. Here, he says, "*I love the Lord because He rescues me from disaster*":

> The cords of death encompassed me
> And the terrors of Sheol came upon me;
> I found distress and sorrow.
> Then I called upon the name of the Lord:
> "O Lord, I beseech You, save my life!" (vv. 3–4)

It's clear that the psalmist isn't just experiencing a passing trial. Look at the terms he uses: "cords of death," "terrors of Sheol," "distress and sorrow," "save my life!" This is a distressing situation. There's no way out! So the psalmist desperately calls out to God for help, and the Lord reaches down to deliver him:

> Gracious is the Lord, and righteous;
> Yes, our God is compassionate.
> The Lord preserves the simple;
> I was brought low, and He saved me. (vv. 5–6)

Notice how God rescues His people. He doesn't reach down, grab us, throw us to the curb, and say, "Now sit there and think about the mess you've made of your life! And don't call on me again until you get yourself straightened out." That would be giving us what we *deserve*. Instead, He reaches out to us at the point of our need, restores us to fellowship with Him, and allows our souls to rest:

> Return to your rest, O my soul,
> For the Lord has dealt bountifully with you.
> For You have rescued my soul from death,
> My eyes from tears,
> My feet from stumbling.
> I shall walk before the Lord
> In the land of the living. (vv. 7–10)

In essence, the psalmist says, "How do I love thee? Let me count the ways. I love You because when I call upon You, You hear me. You rescue me from the depths of my despair. You comfort and forgive me, even when I don't deserve it. You give me rest and keep me safe." What a testimony to the goodness of our God!

In the next two verses, the psalmist recalls how he believed in God during his affliction, when he came to realize his own desperate condition and the complete unreliability of those around him:

> I believed when I said,
> "I am greatly afflicted."
> I said in my alarm,
> "All men are liars." (vv. 10–11)

Interestingly, in the first line of verse 10, Paul quotes from the ancient Greek version of the Hebrew Bible:

> But having the same spirit of faith, according to which is written, "*I believed, therefore I spoke*," we also believe, therefore we also speak. (2 Corinthians 2:14, emphasis added)

Paul sees the psalmist as a model of faith. The psalmist didn't believe in God fully until he faced the truth about his own desperate need and the inability of anyone to help him. When he finally stopped depending on himself and others, then he could truly lean on God. And it was at that point of complete dependency that the Lord rescued him. The psalmist never understood what true devotion to God was until he was forced to rely on Him alone. Out of that end-of-the-rope experience grew the psalmist's deep affection for his Father.

Our Gifts to God

Such passion flowing from the psalmist's soul must find its expression in some tangible way. True love leads to action! So the psalmist asks the question:

> What shall I render to the Lord
> For all His benefits toward me? (v. 12)

Let's ask ourselves the same question: What can we render to Him in return for all the gracious gifts He has given us? What can we possibly offer God, Who has everything? The rest of this psalm lists three particular things that can be given to God.

Praise Him for Our Deliverance

The psalmist uses picturesque language to illustrate his first offering of praise. He rejoices, "*I shall openly declare that the Lord*

91

is my deliverer":

> I shall lift up the cup of salvation
> And call upon the name of the Lord. (v. 13)

We lift our cup high. Why? To publicly praise God. To announce His anointing. To worship Him for His provision. And our cup overflows with something precious—*salvation*. In Hebrew, this word is plural: *salvations*. In the plural, this term is never used to mean *salvation* in the sense of "being born again." Rather, it reflects the numerous times God rescues us from doubt, depression, disappointment, failure, sin, and death.

Keep Our Promises to Him

What else can we offer God in return for His grace and mercy? The psalmist says, "*I shall publicly keep the promises I made to the Lord*":

> I shall pay my vows to the Lord,
> Oh may it be in the presence of all His people.
> (v. 14)

He repeats this sentiment again in verse 18, so it must be important. The private vows and commitments that we make to God are solidified when we demonstrate them in public. We prove our integrity by keeping our promises not only to God, but also to our families and our friends, our co-workers and our neighbors. We show our authenticity and our love for Him when our lives, private and public, overflow with praise and thanksgiving:

> Precious in the sight of the Lord
> Is the death of His godly ones.
> O Lord, surely I am Your servant,
> I am Your servant, the son of your handmaid,
> You have loosed my bonds. (vv. 15–16)

God has a purpose for everything! The psalmist faced imminent death, and God chose to save him. Of course, this is not always the case throughout history. Scripture contains the stories of many martyrs who died for their faith. But God does not let anyone face harm, even death, without a purpose. Our obedience and submission to His will are what He desires, and He promises to reward our faithfulness.

Offer Thanksgiving to Him

What else can we offer God? The psalmist replies, *"I will render to the Lord a humble offering of my gratitude"*:

> To You I shall offer a sacrifice of thanksgiving,
> And call upon the name of the Lord.
> I shall pay my vows to the Lord,
> Oh may it be in the presence of all His people,
> In the courts of the Lord's house,
> In the midst of you, O Jerusalem.
> Praise the Lord! (v. 17–19)

What does God desire? Our humble thanks. Our genuine gratitude. He wants us to announce His praises to the world! How do we love Thee, God? May we not forget to count the many ways You have been good to us and, as the psalmist did, share Your goodness with others.

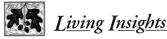 *Living Insights*

Ever heard the phrase "Just do it!"? Nike's multi-million dollar advertising campaign has made this slogan world-famous. Behind this catchphrase are several unspoken exhortations: Leave your excuses in the dust. Achieve your goals. Overcome obstacles. Set aside your fears. Challenge yourself. Test your limits. "Just do it!" takes our ideas and puts them into action. It's where the rubber meets the road.

What about "praise and worship"? It's so easy for us to use this phrase without giving any thought to what it truly means. We discuss it, debate it, write about it, read about it, analyze it, and try to define it. But how often do we honestly *do* it?

Praise should be constantly on our tongues, overflowing from the depths of our souls because of God's incredible love and goodness. Worship should be the attitude of our hearts toward God. He has graciously provided for us and protected us, even to the point of sacrificing His only Son, Jesus Christ, to give us salvation and eternal life. That should cause us to lift up a continual song of praise. So "Just do it!"

Ask yourself the following questions:

Have I experienced problems or circumstances in the past that have robbed me of my joy and lessened my ability to praise God? What were they? How did I deal with them?

_____

_____

_____

_____

_____

Am I currently feeling down, unable to feel a real sense of praise? Have I lost the smiles and laughter that used to characterize my life? If so, what steps can I take to achieve restoration? Who are the people in my life who might be able to encourage and help me?

_____

_____

_____

_____

_____

What can I do right now to start making praise an integral part of my daily life? How can I express my worship to the Lord through the activities of my day? Be as specific as possible. Here are some examples to get you started: I will listen to worship music in my car, at work, and at home. I will talk about God's blessings with my spouse, children, family, and friends. I will read Bible verses that remind me to praise God. I will join the choir or another ministry. I will be more deliberate about telling unbelievers what God has done for me.

_____

_____

_____

_____

_____

_____

_____

_____

_____

 *Questions for Group Discussion*

1. In what ways do you express your love and care for others in your family? How do you show love to your spouse and children? What about to your friends? Your co-workers? Your neighbors? Your small group? Members of your church? What are some steps you can take to more actively encourage and love those people that you see every day?

2. If you were going to write a love sonnet or a song of praise to God, what would it say? What has God done in your life? What blessings have you received from Him? Express your thoughts to God by taking out a sheet of paper and composing a short love sonnet or a song of praise, either individually or as a group. Then, if you wish, share your "creation" with the group.

3. Discuss a time in your life when you, like the psalmist in this chapter, experienced a dark or difficult moment. What happened? How did you feel? How did God restore you? How did you express your gratitude to Him?

4. We hear the word *worship* used in various contexts. Unfortunately, many of these contexts have nothing to do with God! How do you hear this term used in your everyday life? What things are you often tempted to worship besides God? What practical steps can you take to keep these things from becoming idols in your life?

BOOKS FOR PROBING FURTHER

Hopefully, this study has been a source of encouragement to you. More than that, we hope it has sparked your interest in exploring the vast treasure trove of Old Testament passages to discover new inspiration to remain faithful to Christ every day.

We encourage you to continue on this path of discovery by investigating some additional resources. Some of these are general in nature, while others are more specifically related to practical Christianity. As you utilize these resources, we pray that you will continue to know the Lord's favor as you seek Him in His Word!

Bible Study Resources

Bright, John. *A History of Israel: Third Edition.* Philadelphia, Pa.: Westminster Press, 1981.

Hendricks, Howard G. *Living by the Book.* Chicago, Ill.: Moody Press, 1993.

Insight for Living. *Insight's Bible Companion: Practical Helps for Better Study,* vol. 1. Anaheim, Ca.: Insight for Living, 1999.

Insight for Living. *Insight's Bible Companion: Practical Helps for Better Study,* vol. 2. Anaheim, Ca.: Insight for Living, 2000.

Ross, Alan P. *Creation & Blessing: A Guide to the Study and Exposition of Genesis.* Grand Rapids, Mich.: Baker Book House, 1996.

Vos, Howard F. *New Illustrated Bible Manners & Customs: How the People of the Bible Really Lived.* Nashville, Tenn.: Thomas Nelson, 1999.

Interactive Study Resources

Yancey, Philip. *Bible Foundations: An Interactive Journey Through the Old and New Testament.* Grand Rapids, Mich.: Discovery Interactive, 1999.

Books Related to Practical Christianity

Begg, Alistair. *The Hand of God: Finding His Care in All Circumstances.* Chicago, Ill.: Moody Press, 1999.

Colson, Charles. *Kingdoms in Conflict.* Grand Rapids, Mich.: William Morrow and Zondervan Publishing House, 1987.

Crabb, Dr. Larry and Dr. Dan B. Allender. *Hope When You're Hurting.* Grand Rapids, Mich.: Zondervan Publishing House, 1996.

Dillow, Linda and Lorraine Pintus. *Intimate Issues: Conversations Woman to Woman.* Colorado Springs, Colo.: WaterBrook Press, 1999.

Elliot, Elisabeth. *Passion and Purity: Bringing Your Love Life Under Christ's Control.* Old Tappan, N. J.: Fleming H. Revell Co., 1984.

Foster, Richard J. *A Celebration of Discipline.* San Francisco, Calif.: Harper Books, 1988.

Hybels, Bill. *Descending into Greatness.* Grand Rapids, Mich.: Zondervan Publishing House, 1992.

Lutzer, Erwin W. *How to Say No to a Stubborn Habit When You Really Want to Say Yes.* Colorado Springs, Colo.: Chariot Victor Press, 1994.

Mabery-Foster, Lucy. *Women and the Church: Reaching, Teaching, and Developing Women for Christ.* Nashville, Tenn.: Word Publishing, 1999.

Patterson, Ben. *Deepening Your Conversation with God: Learning to Love to Pray.* Minneapolis, Minn.: Bethany House Publishers, 2001.

Wilkinson, Bruce. *Secrets of the Vine: Breaking Through to Abundance.* Sisters, Ore.: Multnomah Publishers, 2001.

Some of the books listed may be out of print and available only through a library. For those currently available, please contact your local Christian bookstore. Books by Charles R. Swindoll may be obtained through the Insight for Living Resource Center, as well as many books by other authors. Just call the IFL office that serves you.

Insight for Living also has Bible study guides available on many books of the Bible as well as on a variety of topics, Bible characters, and contemporary issues. For more information, see the ordering instructions that follow and contact the office that serves you.

NOTES

NOTES

NOTES

ORDERING INFORMATION
PRACTICAL CHRISTIANITY

If you would like to order additional Bible study guides, purchase the audiocassette series that accompanies this guide, or request our product catalogs, please contact the office that serves you.

United States and International locations:

Insight for Living
Post Office Box 269000
Plano, TX 75026-9000

1-800-772-8888, 24 hours a day, seven days a week (U.S. contacts) International constituents may contact the U.S. office through mail queries.

Canada:

Insight for Living Ministries
Post Office Box 2510
Vancouver, BC, Canada V6B 3W7

1-800-663-7639, 24 hours a day, seven days a week
InfoCanada@insight.org

Australia:

Insight for Living, Inc.
20 Albert Street
Blackburn, VIC 3130, Australia

Toll-free 1800 772 888 or (03) 9877-4277, 8:30 A.M. to 5:00 P.M., Monday to Friday
iflaus@insight.org

World Wide Web:
www.insight.org

Bible Study Guide Subscription Program

Bible study guide subscriptions are available. Please call or write the office nearest you to find out how you can receive our Bible study guides on a regular basis.